George Hadfield

The Expediency of Relieving the Bishops from Attendance in Parliament

Illustrated by Episcopal Speeches and Votes in the Irish Church Debates of 1868 and 1869

George Hadfield

The Expediency of Relieving the Bishops from Attendance in Parliament
Illustrated by Episcopal Speeches and Votes in the Irish Church Debates of 1868 and 1869

ISBN/EAN: 9783337250003

Printed in Europe, USA, Canada, Australia, Japan

Cover: Foto ©Lupo / pixelio.de

More available books at **www.hansebooks.com**

THE EXPEDIENCY

OF

RELIEVING THE BISHOPS

FROM

ATTENDANCE IN PARLIAMENT,

ILLUSTRATED

BY EPISCOPAL SPEECHES AND VOTES

IN THE

IRISH CHURCH DEBATES

Of 1868 *and* 1869.

PUBLISHED BY GEORGE HADFIELD, ESQ., M.P.

WITH AN

INTRODUCTORY REVIEW

BY

A MANCHESTER REFORMER.

LONDON:
PUBLISHED BY E. STANFORD, 6 & 7, CHARING CROSS.
MANCHESTER: TUBBS & BROOK, 11, MARKET STREET.
1870.

LEADER AND SONS, PRINTERS, SHEFFIELD.

CONTENTS.

                                                                           PAGE.

INTRODUCTORY REVIEW—
   The Conduct of the Bishops in the Irish Church Debate, 1869. 5

ILLUSTRATIONS

OF THE EXPEDIENCY OF RELIEVING THE BISHOPS FROM ATTENDANCE IN PARLIAMENT.

  I. Address of the Archbishop of Dublin (*Trench*) . . 31
 II. Speech of the Bishop of Peterborough (*Magee*) . . 35
III. Speech of the Bishop of Oxford (*Wilberforce*) . . . 41
IV. Speeches of the Archbishop of Canterbury (*Campbell Tait*) 45
 V. Votes of the Bishops 50
VI. Votes of Catholic Peers 68
VII. Quotations of Churchmen's opinions 70
    CONCLUSION 74

THE CONDUCT OF THE BISHOPS IN THE IRISH CHURCH DEBATE

REVIEWED.

THE position in which the Bishops of the English Church have placed themselves by their speeches and votes, in the late Session of Parliament, when the Irish Church Bill was before the House of Lords, is of the gravest character. It must awaken serious thought, and give rise to anxious questionings, with men of all parties. To many of the best members of their own communion, of different theological schools, their conduct has occasioned both surprise and regret, not unmingled with feelings of shame. Multitudes outside of that communion, who love and maintain the principles of the Reformation with those of an enlightened and free Christianity, beheld their course at the time, and recall it now, with reprobation and disgust. Once again the misfortune has happened to their Spiritual Lordships to satisfy no body of men by their line of action, and to come off from the field of conflict without either the laurels of victory or the sympathy yielded to honourable defeat. The very men who before the struggle gloried in them as the impregnable bulwarks of Protestantism, would now hang down their heads at the mention of their names. They cannot adopt the words of Francis I., after the battle of Pavia, and say,—"All is lost, excepting our honour;" for they have lost everything of consequence for which they contended, and their honour to boot. They have not saved the Irish Church Establishment: they have discredited and endangered their own. The language employed by several of them was insulting to the Government, and the arguments of others outraged the conscience of the people. A measure of justice they denounced as "spoliation"; the provisions of mercy they flouted as a "sham"; while by supporting schemes of concurrent endowment they showed an utter indifference to religious truth. They were ready to bargain for the surrender of the citadel, on condition of winning for their clients a share of the spoils. The proposal was declined by the Roman Catholic party—*without thanks*. The policy and the piety of these Lordly Prelates have been weighed in the balance, and both have been found wanting. Their policy is lacking in all the elements of wisdom: their religious consistency stands discredited and suspected. As for their *dignity*—they freely sacrificed it—perhaps laid it aside as an awkward encumbrance —in the eager scramble for scraps of re-endowment. They stooped to the mortifications of humility, but came short both of the grace and the reward.

These things cannot be recalled without deep sorrow. It must be a grief to all who love the cause of our common Christianity, that it should sustain this injury at the hands of those who are looked up to as its official representatives in the Imperial Senate, by a large proportion of the English people. It stirs the question, as to how it came to pass that reverend and learned men should fall into such serious mistakes, and should evince such a want of sympathy with the prevailing sentiments of the most enlightened and earnest portion of their countrymen, as well as an incapacity of discerning the dangers and embarrassments in which their counsels, if followed, would most certainly have involved us. The occupants of the Episcopal Bench at the present time are undoubtedly, as a body, superior to most of those who in former times have enjoyed that honour. In their own proper department of duty, as Chief Pastors of the Church and guides of the clergy, a large measure of esteem is readily accorded to them, for their learning, their probity, and their religious zeal. But when they are led to step beyond their true province, and, as a part of the Upper House of Legislature, to meddle with the political interests of the empire, then it is that they betray their incompetency, and provoke general censure. Need this occasion any surprise, when we consider their previous training and their habitual associations, and reflect on the wide discrepancy that must always exist between the qualifications which are appropriate to a true Bishop and those which are demanded in a Legislator? But the consequence follows that the strongest objections are now entertained by many faithful members of the English Church to this unhappy mixture of incongruous offices and functions. The presence of the Bishops in the House of Lords has become, not simply an offence to Nonconformists, but an anomaly and an evil which earnest Churchmen deplore and desire to see removed. The time has evidently arrived when this matter is ripe for discussion, and when a movement should be made to bring it into the front rank of the questions of the day. Delay will no doubt intervene before successful action can be taken: so it has been with all great questions of political and social amelioration. But if the experience of the last forty years teaches us anything, it is this, that events hasten on with accelerated speed, and often come with surprise even on those who have been labouring and watching for their accomplishment. Opinion ripens with wonderful rapidity in our day. The opportune conjunction of favourable circumstances anticipates our hopes. While we are as yet only mustering our forces and examining our arms, the hour strikes which summons us to a successful assault on the entrenchments of the foe.

As a contribution to the preparatory work which must precede the removal of the evil in question, it is proposed to take a brief review of the sentiments advanced and the policy advocated by the Bishops, in the recent debates in the Upper House on the Bill for the Disestablishment and Disendowment of the Irish Church. This was a testing occasion, and supplies us with ample materials for forming a decided judgment as to the propriety or advantage of their holding seats in the Legislature. Their Lordships took a very active and prominent part in these debates; which was, indeed, naturally and fairly expected of them. We are thus able to form a more complete estimate of their views and spirit in relation to the momentous interests that were at stake. No one can charge them with reticence or ambiguity. All must admit that their speeches—whatever else may be thought of them—contributed in no ordinary degree to the vigour, the liveliness, and the eloquence of the discussion. But it is not in the light of oratorical or debating talent that we have to study their expressions. We must bring them to the sifting test of such enquiries as the following.

In this great crisis of our national affairs, were they distinguished for giving wise and prudent counsels, tending to avert imminent and exasperating collision? Did they pursue a course which was likely to reconcile opposing parties, and antagonistic branches of the Legislature, as might fairly have been expected from their sacred office and character? Standing, as they do, in a highly privileged position, and representing a Church which prides itself on the gentlemanly bearing of its clergy, did they breathe the spirit of charity and goodwill, and fulfil the claims of Christian courtesy, when speaking of the non-endowed Churches of the country, and of the men whom these Churches honour as their ministers? But, above all, did they so handle the matters in debate as to lift them up from the low level of earthly politics, to the higher region of spiritual principles,—or simply, let us say, of those lofty moral considerations which ought to be habitually present to a Christian mind? Were their views and aims throughout the discussion marked by a superiority to worldliness—to what is narrow and sectarian—to what is petty, selfish, and grasping? Surely if the presence of Christian Bishops be desirable in a political assembly,—or rather, if their absence from their own dioceses and pastoral duties can be at all defended,—it must be in the expectation that advantages like these may be gained, and that the deliberations of our Senate may be elevated and hallowed by the purer atmosphere of thought and feeling which religious persons shall breathe around them. If any such fond expectation were cherished, the procedure of nearly all the Bishops on the occasion on which we are treating, is enough to dispel it for ever.

The conjunction was one of solemn and momentous interest. The time had evidently arrived in the history of the sister island when the unrighteous ascendency of a fractional sect must be abandoned. To sustain it by force, or to buttress it with bribes would no longer avail. Mere palliatives and timid compromises had been tried too long, and must be exchanged for consistent and thorough measures. A new band of statesmen had taken the helm of affairs, unhampered by old traditions, men at once honest and resolute, prepared to carry out their convictions without personal regards, and strong in the support of an enlightened and united majority. The country had been appealed to with the utmost distinctness on the main issue, and had spoken out unmistakably. Men in general felt that the time for delay in the removal of Irish grievances had long passed, and that the most palpable of them all, the most notorious—though not the most oppressive—*the Establishment of an alien Church*—must receive immediate and decisive treatment. We stood before the other nations of Europe taunted and shamed with this crying injustice. It was a perpetual reproach to the name and honour of England. It was the insulting symbol to the Irish people of a wretched policy, pursued through three centuries of misgovernment and oppression, which had disorganized society, driven multitudes into exile, brought the country to the verge of ruin, and made rebellion and assassination chronic and incurable. If a remedy was to be applied to the sufferings of Ireland, a commencement must be made—the ground must be cleared—by the removal of this wrong. That would be the pledge of further and more needful reforms. It would inaugurate a new policy of justice and conciliation, and inspire the hope of a brighter era of genuine union and goodwill.

Under the influence of these views and convictions, Mr. Gladstone and his colleagues brought in their Bill for the disestablishment and disendowment of the Irish Church. Its aim was to introduce religious equality, by placing the different churches on the same level of independence, and thus to allay the animosities created by the State patronage and support hitherto accorded to one. It was a masterpiece of legislation, clear and consistent, comprehensive and compact, carrying out one great idea of justice through its multifarious details with such completeness as to repel criticism and defy amendment. It provided fairly for existing life interests, but contained no unworthy concessions or evasions of principle to meet the requirements of a party. It could not be disintegrated and transformed by skilful manipulation, as some other schemes have been. The wisdom and ability displayed in the manner of its introduction and advocacy, by the Leader of the House and the Attorney-General for Ireland in particular, were truly admirable; while the discipline and self-control of the majority, in silently supporting the Bill, like an unbroken phalanx, against all attacks, were more impressive than the most ardent eloquence. The Bill passed in its integrity, carried by one of the largest majorities that has been seen for many years; and thus, backed by the opinions of the great body of the people, was sent up to the House of Lords.

To the majority of that House it was known to be eminently distasteful, for obvious reasons. Their Lordships are an aristocratic assembly, deeply interested from their constitution and traditions in all that is marked by privilege and monopoly. These features were indelibly stamped on the Irish Church in their strongest form. It was the mere creature and preserve of an aristocratic faction. Could they be expected quietly to abandon it to its fate? A small body of their Lordships, guided by the dictates of an enlightened liberality, and preferring the real interests of the nation to the supposed interests of their order, were prepared to give the Bill their hearty support. They enjoyed the leadership of a nobleman —Earl Granville—who won the admiration of all parties by his conciliatory demeanour, his unfailing tact, and the serenity of temper he maintained under most trying circumstances. The opponents of the Bill were very powerful, both in numbers and in talent, and would fain have got rid of it altogether. This, however, was a questionable and perilous course to take. It could no longer be said with any appearance of truth that the proposed measure involved a surprise, and that an opportunity had not been given to the country at large fairly to weigh its principal issues. In the closing session of the previous Parliament, this had been pleaded as a reason for throwing out the Suspensory Bill, which had passed the House of Commons by a majority of 54. But since then a special appeal had been made on this very question to the enlarged constituencies throughout the three kingdoms. The case had been debated and discussed in every possible way, and the great body of the people had pronounced a decided verdict, which clearly would prove irreversible. The more sagacious portion of the Peers saw that the rejection of the Bill would be a serious mistake; that such a step could only be followed by more intense excitement, and would end in their being compelled to submit to the humiliation of having a more severe and sweeping measure thrust upon them. Thus the Irish Church would receive less favourable terms, and a fatal blow would be given to the dignity and influence of the Upper House. Many of their Lordships, however much they might dislike or even hate the Bill, could not shut their eyes to these obvious considerations. They were therefore prepared to vote for the second reading, and thus to sanction the principle of the measure. But, with one or two exceptions, the bench of Bishops showed themselves utterly blind to what was patent to most other minds, as well as deaf to the voice of justice, and regardless of the peace of the country. Only one of their number (St. David's) had the good sense and the courage both to speak and to vote in favour of the second reading. *Sixteen of them gave their votes against it.* The two Archbishops retired behind the Throne, and abstained from voting, an unconscious indication of the propriety of relieving them from the necessity of taking part in the business of the House. The weight of the Bishops' influence was thus mainly given to a policy which the nation had pronounced unjust, dangerous, and inadmissible, namely, to leave things as they were. They had no counter scheme to propose; they could only cry out against the *sacrilege* of meddling with Church property, forgetful of how that property was acquired, how it had been used by many of their order, and of the iniquity stamped upon it by its long-continued alienation from any ends of national benefit. They did everything in their power to bring the House of Lords into direct and most damaging collision with a popular House of Commons, and to spirit them up to offer a foolish and hopeless resistance to the nation at large. Could anything demonstrate more plainly the utter unfitness of these Prelates to discharge the functions of legislators than the language which some of them used—and which most of them applauded—respecting the relations between the two Houses? Nothing could well be more unconstitutional in spirit, or more revolutionary in its tendency than the sentiments and the counsels which they advocated with reference to the control which the Upper House should claim and exercise in the government of the country. And even since the excitement of the conflict is over, when quiet reflection should surely have supplied sounder conceptions of duty, the Archbishop of Dublin is heard lamenting the defeat which their Lordships have sustained, as if it were the knell of their legislative powers, and venturing the prophecy that it will no longer be possible for them "to thwart the will of the House of Commons in any matter of high national significance." Why, we may ask, was it ever regarded as an admissible course that a majority of the Upper House, representing, not the judgment of the country, but only the personal opinions of certain individuals of the privileged class, should arrogate the right to defeat the policy of her Majesty's responsible advisers, chosen and supported by so large a majority of the national representatives? If views like these were to regulate the counsels of the Peers, we must either come to a dead lock, or should have quietly to resign our liberties into the hands of their Lordships, and treat Parliamentary government as an empty and tedious form.

And this is the service we are to accept from the wisdom and moderation of these Christian Prelates! What an exhibition of reckless audacity was given in the same debate by the Bishop of Peterborough, who, in a style more resembling the declamation of an actor than the serious address of a statesman, harangued their Lordships on the consequences which would befall them if they were induced to pass it in deference to the decisive votes of the Commons. In terms the most exaggerated and puerile, he even taunted them with the degradation and contempt which they would thus bring upon themselves, while he flung out most indecent and insulting reflections on the debates in the other House—a fine specimen truly of the high sense of propriety which we expect in one holding his sacred office. And now, what must be the effect of all this? The House of Peers, under the guidance of wiser heads, not only passed the second reading, but finally —recognising their true position, and adhering to the path of duty and safety—accepted the very details of the measure with slight modifications; and they did this confessedly in deference to the attitude of the other House. If there were then the least shadow of truth in the remonstrances and vaticinations of these right reverend orators, the peerage of Great Britain would now stand weakened and humiliated before the nation. Is not the very reverse the case? Do they not the more enjoy the esteem and confidence of all whose opinion is worth considering, because they frankly yielded to the pressure of a crisis which it would have been madness to brave, and sacrificed their own prepossessions to the judgment of their countrymen? And it is for this that the querulous wailings of Prelatic spleen are poured forth in visitation addresses! The House of Lords may well be congratulated that they will henceforth be freed from the risk of listening to such effusions in their own chamber; and surely on reflection they must feel it desirable that the clearance effected in one part of the Bench were extended to the whole, when it is evident that its occupants have done their best at this time to inflict on the House that diminution of dignity and power which they profess to lament. Whatever else the Bishops may do in the House of Lords, they do not aid it by their sagacity in avoiding those perils to which a hereditary chamber is peculiarly exposed: instead of elevating, they lower its prestige.

So far in reference to the utter want of sound statesmanship displayed by the Spiritual Lords in this debate. But surely we have a right to look to them for much greater qualities. Their proper department is that of religious principle and duty. They should shed the light of higher truth and loftier convictions on the matters in discussion. They should clear away the mist and darkness which earthly and selfish views throw around our path. They should detect and unravel the confusion in which the sophistry of prejudice and personal interest is apt to involve men's minds. It should be theirs to bring measures to the test of the equity and benevolence of the Gospel, and to urge the recognition of "*whatsoever things* are true, whatsoever things are just, whatsoever things are pure, whatsoever things are lovely and of good report." But we should look in vain through their speeches for any distinct, straightforward recognition of principles like these. This, indeed, became an impossibility when they ventured to defend the existence of such an institution as the Irish Church. It excites one's astonishment to observe how they employ all their ingenuity to conceal its real character and working, to elude the true bearings of the question, and to make this monstrous wrong — of which all men but themselves had become ashamed—appear a natural, seemly, and righteous arrangement. Mark the tissue of sophistical evasions in the Bishop of Peterborough's elaborate attempt to meet "the three great issues raised in the debate,"—of the justice of the measure—its policy—and its being in accordance with the verdict of the nation. How does he deal with the noble, Christian-minded appeal of Earl Granville, that we should follow the golden rule of divine morality, and act to Ireland in that way in which, were our situations reversed, we should wish Ireland to act towards ourselves? This argument he takes up, not under the head of *justice*, to which it properly belongs, but under the head of *policy;* and then proceeds to answer it by putting the question—"*Which Ireland do you mean? There is the Ireland of the North, and the Ireland of the South. These are two, and very different Irelands. But, according to my reckoning, there are three. There is a Protestant Ireland; there are the Roman Catholic peasantry of Ireland; and there is—distinct from both, a nation within a nation, owning a separate allegiance—there is the Roman Catholic priesthood. These are the three parties for whom you propose to carry a measure of great State policy.*" Such special pleading as this, on a great question of national justice, is its own refutation. But it is unspeakably painful to remember that this was not the address of some nimble-witted lawyer in a civil court, trying to varnish over a rotten case by dexterous word-fencing, but a high effort of eloquence by a Christian Bishop, before the august assembly of the Peers of England. It is refreshing to turn from such windy and deceptive talk, to the clear, honourable, right-minded reply, by which the following speaker—Earl de Grey and Ripon—completely exposed the sophistry of the Bishop. But if their Spiritual Lordships cannot be trusted to sound a distinct and certain note on the common points of morality;—if they require to be set right there by the sounder understandings, and healthier consciences of the Temporal Peers—what purpose do they serve in that assembly? There is every reason to fear that their participation in such debates does no good to others, and inflicts injury on themselves. They are called to occupy a false position, which blinds and perverts their minds. He is their best friend who advises them to seek release from it speedily.

In spite of the general opposition of the Episcopal Bench, the second reading of the Bill was carried. When the discussion of the clauses began in Committee, it was soon evident, from the amendments proposed by the Opposition, that they were determined, if possible, to rob the measure of everything in it that was vital; and not only to spoil it of all grace, but to transform it from what it professed and was designed to be —an offer of justice and conciliation to the Irish people—into a covert insult and wrong. Having consented to sever the connection of the Church with the State in the sister island, and thus to remove it from its invidious position of supremacy, they wished to give back secretly, in the worst of all forms, what they had professedly taken away. They would have re-endowed this disestablished Church with the greater part, if not the whole, of the property which it had enjoyed before. Where, then, would have been the religious equality which the Bill was intended to establish? This was, in fact, intensifying the wrong complained of, and introducing a new peril. To allow the Church, when no longer under State control, to possess revenues belonging to the nation, is to create an abuse and a danger of the worst kind. The Opposition seemed to have no sense of this. Having adopted the principle of disestablishment, they were bound to carry it out consistently and fairly. Instead of this, they strove in every possible way to make it nugatory. It would be tedious to recount all the expedients by which they strove to filch back what they had nominally surrendered. Let us recall the more glaring instances of encroachment.

In the whole of this tortuous and mischievous policy, they were led on and supported by the Bench of Bishops, who seemed for the time to lose sight of every other consideration than what pertained to the grossest worldly interests. One proposition after another emanated from these Spiritual Lords, which savoured of nothing but extortionate greediness for money. The Bishop of Peterborough proposed that, in the compensation given to holders of benefices, no deduction should be made of the tax on clerical incomes payable to the Ecclesiastical Commissioners; which was claiming for the clergy what had never belonged to them, but had been appropriated by law to public purposes. It was also done in such a way as to conceal the real character of the arrangement. This claim was exposed by Earl Granville; but it was in vain that he showed how complete was its deviation from the principle of the Bill—that it went, in fact, "to the endowment, in a new form, of the disestablished Church,"—and would also act in the most partial manner, immensely increasing the value of larger incomes, but leaving all below £300 unaffected. This most unfair motion was carried by a majority of 44; all the Bishops present, namely, thirteen, voting in its favour in a compact body—as, indeed, they did on every occasion when *more money* was concerned. This may be taken as a specimen of their procedure. It is not needful, as it is certainly not edifying, to go over the other claims they advanced, and which were recklessly conceded; such as retaining the glebe houses **free of building charges, fixing the commutation value of the** incomes of the Episcopalian clergy (not the *Presbyterian*) at fourteen years' purchase, (being an addition of £1,222,000,) and keeping possession of the Ulster glebe lands, granted by James I., out of confiscated estates, under the pretext of their being private endowments. This last unwarrantable appropriation amounted to giving the Church a handsome endowment,—(some said, of a million sterling: but, *deducting* the life interests, it would come to half that sum,) and left her in the Northern part of the island — where the strength of Protestantism is with the Presbyterians— to all outward appearance, in as favoured a position of ascendency as ever, only without the name of State connection. There were several minor additions for which the Bishops pressed, and which the House of Lords voted to give them; but one barefaced piece of extortion, which the Bishop of Peterborough attempted, (July 1st,) was too much even for the Tory Peers; and, at the Earl of Carnarvon's request, the motion was withdrawn. It was nothing less than this: that when the incomes of any of the beneficed clergy fell below £200 a year, they should have compensation given them to that full amount, on the ground of their professional expectations! In short, all through, these reverend dignitaries —whose business it is to teach men to look higher than sordid pelf—seemed, like the insatiable daughters of the horse-leech, to join in one incessant cry of—Give! Give! The issue of their proceedings thus far was apparent in the extravagant provisions of the Bill when it was sent down to the House of Commons. Mr. Gladstone, in his speech on July 15th, put the case thus :—The whole property of the Irish Church— without any addition for the use of the public credit (which greatly augmented its value)—might fairly be reckoned at £15,000,000. The Bill, as it left the House of Commons, dealt so liberally with the Church, that two-thirds of this amount (£10,000,000) were actually surrendered to the condemned institution, or its ministers. (Yet the disendowing clauses were constantly denounced by the Tory Peers and their Episcopal allies, as harsh and niggardly; and the Government was said to be acting towards the Church in the spirit of Shylock.) But the Tory majority in the Lords, inspired mainly by the rapacity and fanaticism of the Bishops —who could not endure the thought of the *secularization of Church property*, as they termed it—had so increased the allowances, that, out of the £15,000,000, the Church positively retained £14,000,000; and this was called *disendowment!* This was to answer the language of the preamble: "*After satisfying, so far as possible, upon principles of equality, as between the several religious denominations in Ireland, all just and equitable claims!*" Seldom has a more impudent farce been transacted under the guise of constitutional legislation. And the most prominent actors in this mixture of farce and factious injustice were the Right Reverend Prelates, who misrepresent the Church of England.

We have no wish to decry or to abuse these ecclesiastical dignitaries. We cheerfully recognize and honour the virtues they display in their proper sphere. But the facts just stated are undeniable and ought not to be forgotten. They grasped, without scruple, at this immense amount of national property, claiming it for their own sect,—now in the name of justice, now in the name of generosity, and now on grounds of pity,—at the very time when the conscience of the nation had been roused to repair a signal and long-continued wrong, by trying, as far as possible, to introduce religious equality in the sister island. That property, which had so long been unrighteously and cruelly alienated from the benefit of the Irish people, the House of Commons tried to restore, at least in part, as a token of penitence and goodwill. The Bishops laid hold of it with their crosiers and snatched it back again, merely giving up the empty shell of State-Establishment. They reversed the miracle of the Hebrew Lawgiver, and instead of sweetening the bitter waters of Marah, they renewed and intensified their bitterness by casting into them the poisonous tree of sectarian selfishness. They cared nothing for the rights and feelings of the Irish people, or for an amicable understanding between them and ourselves. When the bonds of Empire were strained to bursting, and the hearts of men were sick with anxiety for the public welfare, these men thought of nothing—talked about nothing, but glebes and endowments, a larger per centage on commutations, the allowances of rectors and bellringers, deductions for curates and cravings for curtilages—a small slice here and a bigger slice there of the national property, so as to leave as little as possible for the sacrilegious use of the nation itself! Oh it is a sad thing when ministers of religion—or men who should be such—become hucksters in the market of earthly interest, and pedlars in the strife of Parliamentary faction!

It may be said,—they did not crave this money for themselves; they were actuated by sentiments of equity and compassion towards their unfortunate brethren, who were about to be cut adrift from the State. They desired to provision the forlorn bark of the disestablished Church as comfortably as possible, in prospect of the hardships of the voyage that lay before her. The Archbishop of Canterbury seemed to be touched, on one occasion, with a sense of the unseemliness of the attitude which he and his brother Prelates were assuming, in so constantly driving the terms of a good bargain, and hinted at some such apology. But why should the pity of Episcopal bosoms be all lavished on one class of sufferers,—on rectors and curates, with deans and other dignitaries,—and none be left for the poor millions of Ireland, who for three centuries have had no beneficial interest in the national funds? Can this be genuine pity? When a nation lies before us naked, wounded, and heart-sore with the wrongs of centuries, can we excuse Priest and Levite for averting their eyes, and passing by on the other side? Would it be a sufficient defence for this neglect, that they were hastening in pursuit of the robbers; not on purpose to rescue and restore the sufferer's property, but to get a large share of the spoil for some of their own poor brethren? What can have so perverted the minds of these prelates that they could follow such a course without misgiving,—nay, that they could dare so to affront public opinion?

Public opinion, unhappily, has very little hold on Lordly Bishops, in whose appointment the people have no voice whatever—who are merely the irresponsible nominees of a Prime Minister. But the clue to their policy was obvious enough: they were not ashamed to show it. It was nothing less than this: to keep the clergy, as far as possible, from being dependent on the support, and, consequently, amenable to the judgment, of the laity. They regard this arrangement as providing a security for the faithful teaching of the pastors. It simply means that the body of the clergy are to be the despots of the Church, introducing rites, doctrines, and observances, as seems good to their priestly fancies, and so far as they can do it without being checked by the clumsy and expensive machinery of ecclesiastical courts. The Episcopal notion of Church government is to retain the laity—who are *the Church*, if there be a church at all—in a state of perpetual pupilage; always "under tutors and governors;" bound to accept any teaching, or no teaching, that the clergy choose to give them; and to contribute to schemes which they shall not be permitted to control. And it is because the thorough carrying out of "the voluntary principle" would be sure to liberate and elevate the minds of the people, and compel the clergy to show some deference to their judgment, that Episcopal lips seem never weary of decrying, misrepresenting, and vilifying it. Some of them would seem to regard it as David regarded the adversaries of God;—they hate it with a perfect hatred, and count it their enemy. Well, instinct is generally an unerring guide; and the bitter instinctive dislike of our Spiritual Lords to the system of Voluntaryism is no doubt just. Let it come into play, and it would make short work with their dignities. When the Church shall really rest for support, not on legal endowments, but on the free goodwill and offerings of the faithful, there will be an end—not to Bishops as chief pastors —but to Bishops who neglect their dioceses for half the year, that they may oppose the will of the nation, and thwart the progress of sound and Liberal measures from their seats in Parliament. There will be an end also to their baronial titles and honours, to their lavish incomes, and to the extravagant outlay on their Palaces of funds that should have gone to the augmentation of small benefices. Yes; the voluntary principle would make short work of an Episcopal Dives, pleading in his purple and fine linen for some cast-off clothing, to replace the rags of Lazarus, the curate, shivering with his poor children at his gate. Then a stop would be put to such flagrant instances of Nepotism, as those that have recently been reported of the Bishop of St. Asaph (Dr. Short), which are by no means without a parallel. The profitable abuse of Church patronage—so dear to all who live by the smiles of the aristocracy—so fatal to the life and purity of the Church— would cease to be tolerated. Bishops would be obliged to lend a more respectful ear to the petitions of congregations, when remonstrating against novelties introduced in the public service by High Church rectors and vicars. Curates, of course, can be put down at once, and deprived of their licenses; but a beneficed incumbent, who is *independent of the people*, must be treated with the gentlest forbearance. In short, this dreaded voluntaryism would restore their rights to the laity, and make the clergy mindful of their obligations. *Hinc illæ lachrymæ:*—hence this denunciation of the only law of ministerial support sanctioned by Christ and his apostles. How can the Church of England prosper, while she so much resembles the image of Nebuchadnezzar's dream, with a head of gold and feet of clay; her rulers rolling in wealth, her working clergy tramping through the mire of poverty? Quite natural is it that this mitred head of gold should have "a mouth speaking great things," blaspheming voluntaryism, and traducing its ministers.*

The abhorrence of Voluntaryism, displayed by their Lordships, is intensified by their ignorance of its real nature and workings, on which we have not time to dwell, further than to say that—with the facts of our Free Churches before them—there is no excuse for it; and by their lamentable want of all faith in the steady and powerful action of spiritual motives. These men are so surrounded and intoxicated by all the elements and influences of secular dignity and wealth, that they cannot rely on anything that is not tangible and patent to the senses. For a Church to be disestablished and disendowed was, in their view, to be sent adrift on the barren waste of a cold, inhospitable world; it was subjecting her to some wild Colchian experiment of being hewn in pieces and cast into the caldron, in the desperate hope of her coming forth in renovated youth. Do such men believe in anything they do not see and handle? Christian willinghood is nothing in their eyes unless it is backed by a legal document; a Government annuity is the secure bond between a pastor and his work; a glebe house and ten acres of land, free of all charge, are the bulwarks of ministerial fidelity. There is no such thing as Christian manliness in the pastorate—no fear of God—no love to the truth for its own sake, which will induce preachers to speak faithfully to their congregations, unless they have £300 or £400 a year secured to them by law, independently of the people. This is the Episcopal theory of the case—a most wretched and grovelling one indeed. We might ask, Have well-paid rectors and vicars, and courtly bishops, been so very famous for

* See the expressions used by the Archbishop of Canterbury, in his speech on July 22nd, (reported on page 47,) where he describes an unendowed ministry as "the mere servants and tools of those whom they should teach," etc. That is the estimate expressed by the Primate of the English Church of the character and labours of half the Christian ministers in the kingdom, who have done more to advance vital religion than three-fourths of the Established Clergy.

preaching unpleasant truths—truths demanded by the prevalent evils of the day, especially among the upper circles? Is it in Dissenting congregations that the habit of preaching smooth things has been most common? Oh! "tell it not in Gath, publish it not in the streets of Askelon"— this newly announced Episcopal doctrine, that the Church of Christ must not look for fidelity in the pulpit, unless its occupant has an independent income, or at least a good rectory over his head, and a few acres around it! And the men whose minds are so narrow, whose vision is so obtuse, and whose faith is such a poor parasitical plant that it must have some legal prop to cling to, are to occupy a place in the High Council of this Empire as Heads of the Church, and to influence the destinies of the nation! How long is it to be suffered? On what pretence can it be defended? Surely no one can say that they fairly represent in any way the sentiments and wishes of the adherents of the Church of England, when we call to mind the course they adopted in reference to what has been called the scheme of "concurrent endowment." A few words on this head are required in order to complete our review of their procedure.

The motion of the Duke of Cleveland, on July 2nd, and that of Earl Stanhope, brought forward on July 12th, on the third reading of the Bill, had for their object to provide out of the surplus, residences for the clergy and ministers of all denominations, which, as Lord Cairns showed, would really amount to a permanent endowment (in most instances) of £60 a year to each incumbent or parish priest. This would absorb an enormous sum of money, not to speak of the great difficulties in the way of carrying out such an arrangement in the case of any other clergy than those of the Episcopalian Church. But what he and some other Lords on his side of the House especially insisted on was the strong objection to the very principle of such schemes, entertained and expressed by men of all political parties throughout the country; a fact which was notorious. The proposal had been barely mentioned in the House of Commons, and had received no support. It was inconsistent with the principle of the Bill, and with the verdict pronounced by the vast majority of the constituencies in favour of *general disendowment*. It was condemned by all staunch Churchmen and Conservatives, who would not hear of endowing the Roman Catholic clergy. The Roman Catholic members in both Houses most loyally and honourably refused to join in the scheme, as involving a violation of their pledges. It was only the pet notion of a few old Whig peers—political *doctrinaires*—who have been left completely behind by the march of opinion, and whose traditional crotchets are entirely out of date. Earl Harrowby spoke the simple truth when he said (July 12th)—" Nothing is more clear than that, if it had not been stated to the constituencies that endowment of any kind to the Roman Catholic Church was entirely out of the question, we should not have had to go into committee at all, for we should never have had this Bill. If there was one point more than another upon which Conservative seats were lost, and the present majority of the House of Commons was formed, it was the pledge that when the property of the Irish Church was taken away, there should not be an atom of endowment to the Roman Catholic Church." And in those constituencies where the Conservatives, by the aid of the clergy, gained their greatest triumphs,—more especially in Lancashire,—is it not well known that they succeeded by kindling the fire of an ignorant zeal for Protestantism, and charging the Liberal party with a design to advance the interests of Popery? The cry, raised by the clergy in their very pulpits, and which prevailed with too many of their followers, was this: "*Will you have the Queen, or the Pope, to rule over you?*" Mr. Gladstone was constantly defamed and calumniated as a secret favourer of Popery,—as a Jesuit at heart. They encouraged their dupes to look for safety, in this imminent danger which threatened our Protestant institutions, to our *Protestant Bishops;—they*, at least, might be trusted to make no compromise with the emissaries or friends of Rome. And now, how did these same Protestant Bishops act? They not only spoke and pleaded for the scheme of endowing the Roman Catholic priesthood; but on the Duke of Cleveland's motion, (which was lost,) *nine* prelates voted for it, *five* being against; and when Earl Stanhope's motion was carried by a surprise on the third reading, this ill-omened momentary triumph was gained solely by the votes of *seven members of the Episcopal Bench*, among whom were found the two Archbishops, the heads of our Protestant Establishment! What do our Protestant clergy think of that? What do the sound-hearted majority of Churchmen think of it, who desire no fellowship with Rome; who have no love for the nice distinctions which an astute Bishop can make between the *Catholicism* and the *Romanism* of the Popish priesthood? As to the view taken by enlightened and resolute Protestants, like the Scottish people, and the Nonconformists of England and Wales, for that their Lordships may care less; but the time is at hand when it will be brought to bear upon them. It is certainly not a fitting thing that, in a Parliament which legislates for Scotland, Ireland, and Wales, as well as for England, a position of so much dignity and influence should be given to Anglican Bishops, who have no relations or sympathies with the far larger part of the population of the empire, and who have so clearly shown that they are either ignorant or careless of the sentiments held by the members of their own communion on a point of vital concern to the policy of the State.

What could be their inducement to follow this suicidal course? Only two reasons can be suggested, both of which probably had a measure of influence. The scheme aimed a blow at that real religious equality, founded on Voluntaryism, which (as has been remarked) they absolutely hate and dread. It would also secure an additional sum of about £2,000,000 for the Irish Church, while giving only an inconsiderable sum to the other denominations, as was pointed out by Earl Granville. Yet it professed to aim at *religious equality!* Well might that courteous nobleman utter the remonstrance—" Can your Lordships really wish that such a proposal should go down to the other House as illustrative of the spirit of your legislative enactments?" But this remonstrance was thrown away on the Bishops, whose votes carried the motion. Assuredly whatever virtues they may possess, they cannot be commended in Scriptural phrase as being men who *" have understanding of the times, to know what Israel ought to do."* Never was there a scheme mooted more at variance with the prevailing opinions and spirit of the age, or more injurious to the interests both of the Church and of the State.

When this amendment came on for discussion in the House of Commons, it gave occasion to the Irish Roman Catholic members to disclaim in the most emphatic terms any willingness to accept for their clergy either endowments or residences out of the funds of the Irish Church. These gentlemen, as well as the body of the Roman Catholic Peers, certainly acted throughout a most honourable and consistent part, showing the strictest fidelity to their understood engagements with their Liberal allies, for which they are deserving of all praise. Through their firmness the scheme was utterly quashed. Had they shown the slipperiness and subtlety in making convenient distinctions, in which some Episcopal minds excelled, what mischief might have followed!

Nor have we to thank their Spiritual Lordships for averting the serious danger which threatened our national peace when the Bill went back (with their insidious amendments rejected) to the House of Peers. It will not soon be forgotten how nearly we were driven to the brink of a revolutionary crisis on July 20th, by a majority of the Peers insisting on their amendment of the preamble. This really meant *(just what the Bishops had aimed at all along)*—that, sooner than allow the surplus funds of the Irish Church to be devoted to really national objects, they would destroy the Bill itself. *Twelve Prelates, including the three Archbishops, voted in the majority against the Government.* To the credit of the Bishop of Oxford, be it said, he was not the victim of "an unfortunate accident" on this occasion; he was *present in the flesh*, as well as in the spirit, and wisely gave his vote on the Government side. But he stood alone among his brethren, no other Bishop voting in the minority. It was an emergency full of anxiety and peril. A convulsive excitement would soon have followed, and the institutions of the State would have been rudely shaken. The prudence of Lord Cairns, joined with the conciliatory spirit of Earl Granville, and the moderation and forbearance of the very man who had been insultingly taunted with overbearing arrogance, averted the evil. And thus the great healing measure of justice passed at length into an enactment, amidst general congratulations; one great blot on our scutcheon, one fretting sore in Ireland's heart, was removed; and for the first time a policy of disestablishment and disendowment in religious affairs received Imperial sanction.

But now the question arises, *Ought* TWENTY-SIX BISHOPS OF THE ANGLICAN CHURCH *to retain their seats in the United Parliament of Great Britain and Ireland?* So far as they can pretend to represent any party, it is but a doubtful moiety of the English people: the Nonconformists and Roman Catholics, with the majority of the Welsh people, the whole of Scotland, and now Ireland as well, have no part nor lot in them. Yet the political interests of these portions of the empire are seriously affected by the votes of the Bishops; and we have seen how their votes are likely to be given, namely, in general opposition to all Liberal measures. Consistency and sound policy alike demand a speedy reform of this anomaly. Baronial prelates and Episcopal legislators are most undesirable relics of the middle ages. It is evident that the combination of Parliamentary work with their diocesan duties forms a burden which they are not able to bear, and an obligation which they cannot adorn. It is distracting to their minds, injurious to their spirit, and damaging to their reputation. Let them be released from it as speedily as may be. Religion and politics would both benefit largely by the change. It would supersede the necessity for an extension of the Episcopate, and for the appointment of suffragans. It would be the harbinger of a happier era for the country at large, and for the Church of England in particular,—an era when worldly dignities and political functions shall cease to be associated with spiritual offices. Then would she arise in her spiritual strength, cast forth alien elements from her bosom, and become ere long united and free. Then might we look with hopefulness to the time when ascendency shall not be claimed by one communion over others; when the distinctions of social caste between Church and Dissent shall vanish; and when heartburnings and jealousies shall no more separate those who are really one in the faith. Then Religion, shaking off the trammels of State control, and the dust of factious contention, arrayed in purity, and armed with the power of truth, shall go forth as a heavenly minister of peace through the length and breadth of our land.

ILLUSTRATIONS

OF THE EXPEDIENCY OF RELIEVING THE BISHOPS FROM ATTENDANCE IN PARLIAMENT.

I.

THE ARCHBISHOP OF DUBLIN'S *Visitation Address;* referred to on page 13 of the preceding Review.

THE ARCHBISHOP OF DUBLIN (TRENCH), in his Visitation address, in October, thus pronounces his opinion on the humiliation of the House of Lords :—

Referring to the Irish Church Disestablishment Act, he said : " They could not but regret that the House of Lords (although more " for their own sake than for the Church) did not from the first " declare their inability to do anything effectual on our behalf. Had " they avowed from the beginning that they were but the porcelain " jar, and the House of Commons the iron vessel, and that a colli- " sion between the two must at any sacrifice be avoided, one might " have regretted that their real power was not more commensurate " with that which the *theory* of the constitution assigned to them ; " but none could have been so unreasonable as to find fault with " the weak for owning themselves such. It was a pity they promised " so much, and performed so little. *It excited a painful surprise to* " *see the manner in which the House of Lords gave way, amid the* " *mutual congratulations of its members, and as though they were ac-* " *complishing a feat the most glorious; everybody extolling everybody* " *else; the consciousness of having extricated itself from a position of* " *embarrassment rousing in it a delight intense enough to swallow up* " *every thought of the poor Irish Church, at the expense of which this* " *extrication had been effected.*"

" As I live over again," said his Grace, " that memorable night, " I feel that it is not we who have lost and suffered the most." *He* was bold to prophecy that the struggle on the Irish Church Bill would be the very last in which the House of Lords would ever venture even to appear to cross or thwart the will of the House of Commons in any matter of high national significance.

The most Reverend Prelate tells his story with admirable simplicity and truthfulness. It is interesting to learn from such authority the feeling and sentiment in the House of Lords as soon as the Leader for Government announced his intention to proceed no further with the Bill, when the Lords insisted on their amendments in opposition to the House of Commons, and thus brought the two Houses into collision.

The Archbishop of Dublin exhibits an ignorance of the constitution that is surprising, after all that has been done by constitutional means to carry a measure of policy and justice.

In 1868 the House of Commons decided to disestablish and disendow the Church of Ireland, and passed a Suspensory Bill by a majority of 312 to 255.

That Bill was rejected by the House of Lords on the 29th June, by a majority of 192 to 97.

By the advice of a Conservative Government, the Queen appealed to the country and dissolved Parliament. The electors returned a majority of members to the House of Commons, numbering 120, to carry out the measure.

In consequence, the Conservative Government resigned on the 9th December, and the Queen commanded Mr. Gladstone to form a new Government, which he accomplished, and brought a Bill into the House of Commons to disestablish and disendow the Irish Church. The Conservatives opposed the measure, but the House confirmed it in 25 divisions on the second reading and on details; and the Bill was finally read a third time, (31st May,) by a majority of 361 to 247, and sent to the House of Lords.

On the 10th June, 1869, the House of Lords adopted the Bill, and read it a second time by a majority of 179 to 146.

Then followed in the House of Lords 14 divisions, on details, in the committee, on report, at the third reading, and on consideration of amendments rejected by the Commons.

On these occasions the majority of the House of Lords, under

Lord Cairns, their acknowledged leader, showed their opposition to the Government, (for whom the Earl Granville conducted the Bill,) and the solemn decisions of the House of Commons.

So capricious were the Conservative Peers, that they decided to continue the Irish Bishops in the House of Lords for their lives, after the disestablishment of the Irish Church; but this amendment they subsequently cancelled of their own free will.

They changed the time for disestablishing from 1st January, 1871, to 1st January, 1872, and this they changed again to 1st May, 1871; but this amendment was rejected in the House of Commons, and the original clause was restored and adopted by the Lords.

They rejected the Duke of Cleveland's motion for endowing the Catholics and Irish Presbyterians, (2nd July,) by a majority of 146 to 113; but they subsequently (12th July) adopted Earl Stanhope's motion to set aside the resolution of 2nd July, and to endow these denominations, by 121 to 114, being a majority of 7, obtained by the votes of seven Protestant Bishops, and in the absence of thirty-two peers who voted in the majority of 2nd July.

"I am painfully conscious that the Government does not possess the confidence of your Lordships," said Earl Granville; and he patiently bore defeat after defeat, until the Bill became so changed as to be unacceptable to the House of Commons, and that House decided by large majorities to reject all material changes in it that had been made by the House of Lords.

When Earl Granville (20th July) proposed that the House of Lords should not insist on the first of their amendments, the Government was defeated by a majority of 173 to 95.

His Lordship then stated he could proceed no further with the Bill until he had consulted his colleagues, and the debate was adjourned for 48 hours, viz., from Tuesday to Thursday.

This righteous *menace*, from an accomplished and courteous statesman, the Government Leader in the House of Lords,—after exhausting every constitutional effort to pass a just law, on which the peace and satisfaction of Ireland depended,—could not be, and was not, misunderstood.

The House of Lords quailed under it, and succumbed to the House of Commons.

No time was to be lost. The Leader of the Opposition, Lord Cairns, after a supposed consultation with the Leader of the Opposition in the House of Commons, requested an immediate interview with Earl Granville, and capitulated on terms of abandoning every amendment that affected the integrity of the Bill. "I look on these "amendments less as a compromise than as an unconditional sur- "render," said Mr. Vance in the House of Commons; and the Archbishop of Dublin asserts, "The House of Lords will never "again venture to thwart the will of the House of Commons in any "matter of high national significance."

For this result the House of Lords are much indebted to the English and Irish Bishops, and to no one of them are they more indebted than to the Archbishop of Dublin, except it be the Bishop of Peterborough.

His Grace the Archbishop of Dublin voted against the second reading of the Irish Church Bill.

For the Archbishop of Canterbury's motion to enlarge the time for disestablishment to a second year.

For the Bishop of Peterborough's motion, 1st July, 1869.

For additional glebe lands; Earl of Carnarvon's motion.

For the Marquis of Salisbury's motion, for more endowment.

He did not vote against Catholic endowment, on either motion, having absented himself from the divisions.

He voted for the Archbishop of Canterbury's motion, for additional glebe lands to be given to the clergy, (5th July,) estimated at one million.

For Lord Cairns' motion against appropriating the surplus for secular purposes.

Against the Marquis of Clanricarde's motion (9th July).

Absent at the Earl of Devon's motion, (12th July,) to rescind the resolution to continue the seats of Irish Bishops for life.

He voted (20th July) to insist on the Lords' Amendment for altering the preamble of the Bill, which drove the two Houses into collision, and brought on the result before referred to.

Finally, he opposed (22nd July) Earl Granville's motion, not to insist on the amendments to clause 27 (ecclesiastical residences); he divided the House of Lords on it, and was defeated by 47 to 17.

His Grace's "*theory*" of the constitution seems to be that a majority of hereditary and irresponsible Peers, aided by 30 Bishops, should control the Queen's Government, the decision of the House of Commons, and the opinions of the electors of the United Kingdom, expressed at a general election, which drove a Conservative Government from office.

It is consolatory to know that, on and after 1st January, 1871, his Grace's voice and vote in the House of Lords will be known no more for ever.

II.
THE BISHOP OF PETERBOROUGH'S SPEECH.

"The BISHOP of PETERBOROUGH placed himself at one step in "the first rank of Parliamentary orators by a brilliant declamation "against the Bill, marked by every rhetorical merit *except an appre-* "*ciation of the conclusive reasons which have satisfied the country, the* "*House of Commons, and almost every Statesman in England.*— (*Times*, 11th August).

The speech was delivered in opposition to the second reading of the Irish Church Bill, the 15th June, 1869, and deserves consideration in connection with the visitation address of the Archbishop of Dublin, delivered after the Bill had passed into an Act.

In the speech of the Bishop of Peterborough he forewarned the House of Lords of the consequences that would befall them if they passed the Bill, and the Archbishop of Dublin has recorded the result of what has happened to them by enacting the Bill.

As the speech occupied several hours in delivery, we have space only for a very few extracts from this " brilliant piece of declamation."

The following comprises the Bishop's opinion of the two Houses of Parliament, and the character of their debates, viz. :—

" There is one great encouragement I feel—it is a thought that " has been present to my mind all through this debate—that is, that " I have the privilege of addressing an assembly in which freedom of " speech is still permitted to its members. I have heard much, my " Lords, since I had the honour of being a member of your Lord-

"ships' House, and I have read something about the antiquated pre-
"judices which still haunt it, but which are not to be found in the
"other House; but among those antiquated prejudices *I rejoice to
"see that your Lordships still retain the notion that a deliberating
"assembly should be allowed to deliberate.* I have no fear, my
"Lords, at least upon this point, that if the remarks which I venture
"to make should be distasteful to some of your Lordships, I shall be
"at least free to make them. I am reminded that your political
"education is imperfect, but I am glad to find *that you have not
"yet adopted the most recent form of Parliamentary clôture,
"which simply consists in* HOWLING DOWN *the person who takes
"the unpopular side of a debate.* (Oh! Oh!) I regret that in
"the first few words I have spoken I should have called forth
"expressions of dissent; but *I think I am justified in describing
"what I think I saw and heard in what I do not venture to call
"another House, but a public meeting, in which there were present
"a great many Members of Parliament."*—(*Hansard*, 15th June,
page 1854).

This unusual mode of debating in the House of Lords by
slandering the Representatives of the People assembled in the
House of Commons, was not only tolerated, but it was cheered to
the echo, and resulted in the humiliation of the House of Lords in
the eyes of the people.

It was sure, however, to receive some notice in the House of
Lords, and on the 17th June (debate on Mr. Bright's letter)—

EARL GRANVILLE said: "May I not then feel a little regret
"that the Right Reverend Prelate in a speech, the brilliancy of
"which it is perfectly impossible to exaggerate, should have begun
"at a time when the noble and learned Lord's (Lord Cairns) words
"are so true, *even before he was warmed by that great eloquence
"which he possesses, by saying, amid the cheers of the leading
"Bench opposite,* that the House of Commons had 'HOWLED DOWN'
"every attempt to argue against the Bill."

The BISHOP of PETERBOROUGH promptly rose and said: "I
"feel compelled to interrupt the noble Earl. I did not say that
"the House of Commons had 'HOWLED DOWN' any person. *What
"I said was, in that House certain persons were* HOWLED DOWN.

"(Oh! Oh!) That is a very different thing. I take it that the acts of the House of Commons are the collective acts of the whole body. *I did not use the words, 'House of Commons,' in my speech at all, nor did I say or mean that the House of Commons had* HOWLED *any person down. I did say that certain persons in the House of Commons had* HOWLED *down certain speakers.*"—(*Hansard*, 17th June, page 14).

We leave this explanation to be construed by those who may be pleased to compare it with the first report.

The BISHOP of PETERBOROUGH thus describes the Bill introduced by the Government, and adopted in the Houses of Parliament by great majorities, approved by the Queen, and now become the law of the land, viz.:

"Throughout its provisions, this Bill is characterised by a *hard* and *niggardly* spirit. I am surprised by the *injustice and impolicy* of the measure, but I am still more astonished at its intense *shabbiness*. It is a small and pitiful Bill. It is not worthy of a great nation. This great nation in its act of magnanimity and penitence has done the talking, and has put the sackcloth and ashes on the Irish Church, and made the fasting be performed by the poor vergers and organists."—(*Hansard*, 15th June, page 1874).

Brave words these, my Lord Bishop!—especially in view of the following facts: At the census of population in Ireland (1861) the people numbered 5,764,543, and of these the established Episcopal Church comprised 678,661, or *less* than *one-eighth*.

Estimating the property of the late Established Church of Ireland at sixteen millions, the sum appropriated to compensate for life and other interests will exceed eight millions, or *one-half* for the benefit of *one-eighth* of the population.

The Bishop considers this to be shabby, niggardly, unbecoming, and unworthy of a great nation!!!

Let us now take the Right Reverend Prelate's *Prediction of the humiliation of the House of Lords.*

The following passage in the Bishop's speech may excite, in his mind, regret that he uttered it, but it foretold a state of things which the Archbishop of Dublin assures us has actually occurred.

"My Lords, I have but one or two more words to say. I will say
"but a few words, my Lords, about the *menaces* and the *warnings*—
"the mixed menaces and warnings—which have been addressed to
"your Lordships' House by many without, and, so far at least as
"warning is concerned, by some within. My Lords, *I myself* have
"been told that I should be very heedful of the way in which *I*
"*may vote* on this question, *because none may say what will be the*
"*consequences to your Lordships' House*—to the fate of your Lord-
"ships' Order, and to the great interests of the country—of the
"vote you are about to give.

"My Lords, as far as menaces go, I do not think that it is
"necessary that I should say one word by way of inducing your
"Lordships—even if I could hope to induce you to do anything by
"words of mine—to resist those *menaces*.

"I believe that not merely the spirit of your Lordships, but
"your Lordships' high sense of the duty which you owe to the
"country, would lead you to resist any such intolerant and over-
"bearing menaces as those which have been uttered towards you.
"*I believe that if any one of your Lordships were capable of yielding*
"*to those menaces, you would be possessed of sufficient intelligence to*
"*know how utterly useless any such* HUMILIATION *would be in the way*
"*of prolonging your Lordships' existence, as an institution; because*
"*it would be exactly the case of those who, for the sake of preserving*
"*life, lose all that makes life worth living for: it would be an abne-*
"*gation of all your Lordships' duties for the purpose of preserving*
"*those powers which a few years hence would be taken from you.* Your
"Lordships would then be standing in this position in the face of the
"*roused and angry democracy of the country, with which you have been*
"so loudly menaced out of doors, and so gently and tenderly warned
"within. You would then be standing in the face of that fierce and
"angry democracy, with these words on your lips: Spare us, we entreat
"and beseech you! spare us to live a little longer as an Order, is
"all that we ask, so that we may play at being statesmen;—that we
"may sit upon red benches in a gilded House, and affect and pretend

" to guide the destinies of the nation, and play at legislation. Spare
" us for this reason; that we are utterly contemptible, and that we are
" entirely contented with our ignoble position. Spare us for this
" reason; that we have never failed in any case of danger to spare our-
" selves! Spare us, because we have lost the power to hurt any one!
" Spare us, because we have now become the mere subservient tools in
" the hands of the Minister of the day,—the mere armorial bearings
" on the seal that he may take in his hands, to stamp any deed, how-
" ever foolish, and however mischievous! And this is all we have to
" say by way of plea for the continuance of our Order. My Lords,
" I do not believe that there is a Peer in your Lordships' House, or
" any one who is worthy of finding a place in it, who could use such
" language, or think such thoughts; and therefore I will put aside
" all the menaces to which I have referred."—(*Hansard*, 15th
June, page 1874.)

This brilliant passage in a speech that was said to have been
" rarely equalled, and never surpassed," literally produced no effect
whatever on the division, which resulted as follows:

For the Second Reading: Contents.................... 179
         Not Contents............. 146
            Majority......... 33

The House of Commons disallowed every amendment of their
Bill in the House of Lords that in any material way affected it,
and returned it to the House of Lords to be rejected, or to be shorn
of the amendments which had been so ungraciously introduced
into it.

We have already stated the result.

The Bill, as passed by the House of Commons, has now become
the law of the land.

The Bishop of Peterborough foretold what would be the issue
to the House of Lords if they listened to the menaces and warnings
held out to them. He probably heard Earl Granville's menace to
withdraw the Bill, and witnessed its effect on the House of Lords.
He held his peace. And the Archbishop of Dublin has informed us
that what he (the Bishop of Peterborough) foretold, has actually
occurred, by the Peers yielding to the menace.

A word more on the BISHOP's Speech. Shall we regard it as a fair instance of the way in which a Spiritual Physician appointed by the State, pours the healing balm into the wounds of his distracted country?

Here is the peroration of this specimen of Irish eloquence, uttered in the House of Lords, " the first assembly in the world; " but more fitting for a schoolboy contending for a prize at Christmas.

" My Lords,—I hear a great deal about the verdict of the
" nation on this question, but without presuming to judge the con-
" science or the wisdom of others, and speaking wholly and entirely
" for myself, I desire to remember, and I cannot help remembering
" this, that there are other and more distant verdicts than the verdict
" even of this nation, and of this moment, which we must every one
" of us face, at one time or another, and which I *myself am thinking*
" *of* while I am speaking, and in determining upon the vote I am
" about to give. There is the verdict of the English nation in its
" calmer hours, when it may have recovered from its fear and its
" panic, and when it may be disposed to judge those who too hastily
" yielded to its passions. *There is the verdict of after history,* which
" *we* are making even as *we* speak and act in this place, and which is
" hereafter to judge us for our speeches and for our deeds. And, my
" Lords, there is that other more solemn and more awful verdict
" which we shall have to face; and I feel that I shall be then judged
" not for the consequences of my having made a mistake, but for
" the spirit in which I have acted. And, my Lords, *as I think of*
" *the hour in which I must face that verdict*, I DARE NOT, I CANNOT,
" I MUST NOT, AND I WILL NOT, vote for this most unhappy, this
" most ill-timed, this most ill-omened measure, that now lies on
" the table of your Lordships' House."—(*Hansard*, 15th June, page 1877.)

The Bishop accordingly voted against the second reading, and in most of the divisions in the House of Lords which defeated the Government.

The following is a list of his subsequent votes:

He voted for the Archbishop of Canterbury's motion, 29th June.

For Clerical Exemption, (his own motion,) 1st July.

For the Earl of Carnarvon's motion, 1st July.

For the Marquis of Salisbury's motion, 2nd July.
For Catholic and Irish Presbyterian Endowment, 2nd July.
For   ditto   ditto   12th July.
For the Archbishop of Canterbury's motion for increase of glebe lands for the clergy.

Against the Marquis of Clanricarde's motion, 6th July.

Against the Earl of Devon's motion to rescind clause to continue the Irish Bishops in the House of Lords, 12th July.

Against Earl Granville's motion, not to insist on the amendment of the Preamble, which was defeated, and brought the two Houses into collision.

Earl Granville's menace (20th July) silenced the Bishop of Peterborough, and he neither spoke nor voted on the subject of this Bill afterwards.

III.
THE BISHOP OF OXFORD'S SPEECH.

2nd July, 1869.—On the Duke of CLEVELAND's Motion to Endow the Catholics and Irish Presbyterians.

The BISHOP OF OXFORD said: "I venture to ask your Lordships to allow one of the Bench on which I sit to say a very few words in explanation of the vote I am about to give. In voting, as I intend to do, for the amendment of the Noble Duke (the Duke of Cleveland), I cannot profess that I do so with any desire whatever of advancing the Roman Catholic Priests of Ireland. But I think there are three very important points to consider, and I earnestly desire your Lordships to consider them. They are these: That in the Roman Catholic faith there is, first, the element of *Catholicism*, and, secondly, the element of *Romanism*. As far as you promote the power of the teachers of that faith by promoting the element of Catholicism, you strengthen them in the work which you desire they should do. *As far as you help them to set forward the peculiar views which, over and above Catholicism, divide their teaching from the teaching of the early Church, you make them the great legionaries of Romanism in the land.* I believe that by giving to the Roman Catholic priesthood in Ireland the status and position of holding these glebe houses independently, *you will enable them to maintain for themselves a liberty of teaching, which it is of the utmost importance that they should be enabled to pursue.* And therefore it is, and not because I have any sympathy with the peculiarities of their teaching, that *I heartily desire to help them out of the sectional difficulties of their position into something like a grander and more general teaching of Christianity.* And as far as that portion of the subject goes, I *shall give my vote* FEARLESSLY *and openly for giving them these glebes.* I do not think this is a question of con‑ current endowment at all. You have a certain surplus, and in bestowing a portion of it in this way you are not endowing any particular form of Christianity. The evil of so doing lies in making it the paid servant of the State from year to year. *What do you do by this proposition more than you have done with regard to Maynooth?* You are winding up the question once for all, and you are not crea‑ ting any fund for the sustentation of a particular religion. It is said that the sum proposed to be given is large; but, after all, what is it you are taking from the £8,000,000 of Church property? It seems to me, therefore, that this is a question your Lordships ought to settle. The noble and learned Lord (Lord Cairns) talked about the importance of this House leading the opinion of the country by speeches, and not by votes. But when were Englishmen ever led by words, unaccompanied by deeds? It has always been said that the difference between the English and other armies was that the ordinary officer said, "Gentlemen, go on," while the English officer said, "Gentlemen, FOLLOW ME." In the same way, your speeches here may be as loud as you like, but you will not carry public opinion with you unless you show that you have the *courage* to follow up your words by the necessary action. If that is the case, it seems to me that we have at this moment the duty set before us of showing that *we are not afraid of doing that which we believe to be right.* I make the greatest possible allowance for the Government for not proposing such a measure as this. All govern‑ ments must be subject to a certain gentle pressure. *I believe that the convictions of every noble lord upon the Ministerial Bench are with me in this matter;* but they are not able to *march* with us unless they receive a *gentle pressure,* to which I believe they will *yield with the greatest possible satisfaction.* I believe that the country at large, after a very short space of time, will agree with you in the justice of this measure. For what is it you are going to do? *The question is not between the Church of Ireland and these competing religious bodies. If it were, however bigoted I may be thought for saying so, I would not give one single halfpenny of the Church's money to any competing sect.* The question is, when you have created a considerable surplus of money, whether you are to give it to the Roman Catholics, not as an endowment, but in a form which will give to the Roman Catholic priest, and the Presbyterian teacher, a certain independence, which will lift him above the position in which he is at present? It is on this ground that I venture to say, in common with every statesman for these many years past who has dared to state his opinion on this subject, that I believe you will, in passing this amendment, be doing an act of *consummate policy*, as well as of the greatest justice, in so administering these remaining funds."

Division: Contents............ 146
  Not Contents...... 113
  Majority... ...... 33 against Endowment.

The Bishop of Oxford showed no want of courage. A brave British soldier he would have made. Nature designed him for the army, but he devoted his genius and valour to the service of the Church. "Follow me," was the command of this Episcopal hero, and he led eight Bishops into the division lobby, who voted with him for Catholic and Presbyterian endowment, to the astonishment of the House and the country. By a majority of 33, Government successfully resisted the motion, and in this majority were included seven Catholic Peers, while in the minority there were nine Protestant Bishops.

The motion of Earl Stanhope, on 12th July, made in the absence of 32 Peers who had voted against endowment on this occasion, reversed this decision by a majority of *seven Bishops*, who again voted for Catholic and Presbyterian endowment, but this amendment, thus carried in the House of Lords, was rejected in the House of Commons without a division.

The Bishop boldly asserted "his belief that the convictions of every noble Lord upon the Ministerial Bench were with him in this matter." With "a gentle pressure," he believed, "they would yield with the greatest possible satisfaction." It is to be regretted he did not express the grounds he had for this monstrous assumption. The country will not believe, without evidence, in the insincerity and hypocrisy of the Ministers of the Crown.

An explanation should have been given as to whom the Right Reverend Prelate referred to, when he spoke of "competing bodies," to whom "*he would not give one single halfpenny of the Church's money.*" He cannot include in these "competing sects" either the Catholics or the Irish Presbyterians, because his Lordship voted to give them two millions of the Church's property. In the House of Commons no one obtained "one single halfpenny" of this property for any sect or body, or for religious endowment in any shape or form whatever, except what has been embodied in the Act of Parliament.

The Bishop must hold peculiar views on other things besides theology, for he believed that by the passing of the Duke of Cleveland's amendment, the House of Lords would be doing an act of CONSUMMATE POLICY, as well as of the *greatest justice*. And yet it was clear that the object of that amendment found no favour with the Roman Catholics, and (if carried) would certainly have raised a storm of indignation throughout the country. His Lordship's courage may be great, and his mental subtlety unequalled, but we must take leave to question his wisdom.

But though he could not see what was best for the nation, he had a keen eye to what was safest for himself. When the crisis came, on July 20th, he alone of the Bishops, like a *faithful Abdiel*, voted with the Government. For this Episcopal Abdiel—though he cannot look up for guidance to the steadfast stars—can see as high as the vane of the steeple, and mark which way the wind blows. Alas! that in this plausible, wily priest we must own the son of the great and good William Wilberforce.

IV.
THE ARCHBISHOP OF CANTERBURY.
2nd July, 1869.—On the Duke of Cleveland's motion.

The ARCHBISHOP of CANTERBURY.—"It is quite impossible for me to give my vote without saying a few words, the more so as I do not quite agree with my Right Reverend Brother (the Bishop of Oxford) in the reasons which guide his vote on this question.

"My reason for supporting the amendment of the Noble Duke (the Duke of Cleveland) is this, that ever since I was able to think on politics, I have conceived that the policy indicated by the noble Earl (Earl Russell), who lately addressed the House, was the only policy likely to bring peace to Ireland. I have in my humble way supported that policy in matters of education. I have supported it in the matter of the Queen's Colleges. I have always thought it right and fair that the Maynooth Grant should be made. I have thought that although we were not bound in Ireland, as in Canada, by an actual treaty, yet, being brought into close relations with our Roman Catholic brethren, we could not deny them that small meed of justice which the Maynooth Grant gave them, without treating them as if they were our slaves. Therefore, when an opportunity occurs—unexpectedly to me, not willingly—and I am called upon to say whether I still maintain the policy which I have always supported, I am constrained to adhere to the opinions which I have entertained for the last twenty years. In doing so, I am consoled by the thought that, after all, there is no difference in principle, though there is considerable difference in policy, between the two proposals before the Committee. And, upon the whole, as the Noble Marquis (the Marquis of Salisbury) said, I prefer making a respectable secular priest comfortable in his house to paying an indefinite number of monks and nuns for services in lunatic and other asylums, and think that the amendment supports that form of Romanism which is the least objectionable. I believe the day has passed long ago when you could say that you did not recognise the existence of Romanism in Ireland. I believe I am not wrong in saying that a fair salary—two-thirds above that given to any Protestant clergyman—is given in every union in

Ireland to the Priest out of the poor rate. And I think that this is just, because a vast majority of the poor are Roman Catholics; they must be attended to by somebody, and as they cannot be attended to by the Protestant clergyman, the Roman Catholic priest must be employed and paid for his services. I know also that this mode of paying the chaplain of the workhouse really provides a Roman Catholic curate in a very large number of parishes in Ireland, because the priest has a salary far larger than is required for his service in the workhouse, and the greater part of his time is spent in teaching Roman Catholics who are not in the poorhouse. This being the case, it appears to me to be something not very real to say that there is a great principle at stake in an amendment which proposes to put the Roman Catholic priests into comfortable dwellings. The only thing that makes one hesitate to do this, is that the money, unlike the money in the case of the workhouses, and unlike that which used to be voted for Maynooth, comes out of the funds of the Irish Church. Still, it must be remembered that the money is to be taken from the Church and applied to Irish purposes. Being forced to pronounce an opinion between what seems to me *the sham scheme* proposed by the Government as to the disposal of the surplus, and the real scheme of the Noble Duke, I shall record my vote in favour of the latter."

Extracts from His Grace's Speech on the Commons' Amendments,
22nd July, 1869.

" I still regard the sacrifice of an Established Church in Ireland as a great misfortune. I hold as strongly as ever that the right policy for Ireland would have been to maintain the Established Church there in moderate proportions, and to give the people of Ireland the benefit which the sanction of religion by the State must confer upon a nation. To say anything more, however, on that point, would be to go back to the principle of the second reading of the Bill, and to call in question the decision of the House. But when the Established Church was gone, it still remained for us to consider whether we ought not to endeavour, as much as possible, to maintain an endowed Church: and I am thankful to believe that, by some means or other—in truth, not in name; because we are not allowed to mention such a thing as endowment—we shall be able to maintain an endowed Church of a very moderate character. These endowments, I grant, may be small, and the Church will have great difficulties to contend with; but I regard the possession of these endowments as a matter of great importance for the religious, social, and political well-being of Ireland. The evil of an unendowed clergy is confessed by all. * * * All men who understand what the office of the clergy is, greatly deplore the fact that, when they are so stripped of all endowments, they become *the mere servants and tools of those whom they should teach.* Whether, therefore, it is to be called endowment or not, I am thankful that, through some means or other, there is to be retained something, which is to be placed in the hands of a Church body, for the benefit of the Church of Ireland, to carry on its ministrations independently of the offerings of the congregations. * * * I think, therefore, all experience proves that it is a great religious question, whether or not the clergy shall be entirely dependent on their flocks for their subsistence: and I am thankful to believe that if this bill passes, according to what I am willing to say are the conciliatory proposals of the Government, though they may not be satisfactory to all, something will remain secured as a means of subsistence for the clergy of the disestablished Church of Ireland. It has been remarked in the course of these debates, that the religion is not worth preserving which looks to the secular arm, or the mere prop of pecuniary endowment, for its maintenance. Now, our religion requires nothing of the kind; but it is quite possible that if we should neglect opportunities of good, which God has given us, our religion may not be presented to the people in the purest form. I believe that evil will be averted in Ireland; partly, I trust, by the fact that some endowment will still be left for the clergy, and still more by the fact that the clergy who will first have to administer the concerns of that Church will have been brought up in a totally different system from the voluntary system. *If they had had to start on this voluntary system, I should have despaired for the religion, for the social improvement, and for the political security of the country;* but, bred as they have been, in a totally different system, educated, trained in habits of intimacy with the clergy of the English Church, and commanding, as they do, even from a Roman Catholic Prelate, that tribute to their honour which has been more than once quoted 'elsewhere,' and which shows that they are quite unlike those fostered on the voluntary system, I believe they will be able, if any men can, to import into this Free Church something of that spirit which they have learned in a nobler, higher, and far better system. I will conclude by reading the words in which that Roman Catholic Prelate bears his testimony to the Irish clergy; and which I trust will still remain characteristic of them, and distinguish them from *all persons who live by pandering to the passions of the people:*

"In every relation of life, the Protestant clergy who reside among us are not only blameless, but estimable and edifying. They are peaceful with all, and to their neighbours they are kind when they can; and we know that on many occasions they would be more active in beneficence, but that they do not wish to appear meddling, or incur the suspicion of tampering with poor Catholics. In bearing, in manners, and in dress, they become their state. If they are not learned theologians, they are accomplished scholars and polished gentlemen." &c.

We have here some most extraordinary sentiments to be held and professed by the Head of a great Christian community. In his Grace's present state of health, delicacy forbids us to do more than simply to notify the following points.

1. The proposal to appropriate funds to "the relief of unavoidable calamity and suffering"—for which at present most insufficient provision is made—is "a SHAM scheme." To give the money to clergymen and priests, preaching opposite and contradictory doctrines, is *Real* beneficence and excellent policy.

2. The support of the Christian Ministry by the endowments of the State,—which leads inevitably to patronage, with all its abuses, and deprives the Church of all liberty of action, as well as of discipline,—is "*a nobler, higher, and far better system*" than the Apostolic law, "*Let him that is taught in the word communicate unto him that teacheth in all good things.*"

3. If a Church were compelled to start on the VOLUNTARY SYSTEM,—that is, *to depend simply on the sense of Christian obligation, the living piety,* and *the grateful liberality of its members,*—it would

incline the Most Reverend Archibald Campbell Tait to *despair for the religion, for the social improvement, and for the political security* of the country where that Church undertook to labour. Yet on that system the Christian Church began, and in her best and purest times has known no other.

Lastly, all ministers that have not been trained under the Establishment are marked by an inferior spirit and style of character, and are tempted to " *live by pandering to the passions of the people.*"

The only reply we make is this. May his Grace's health be speedily restored, and may the Divine goodness strengthen him and spare him for many years, that he may with calmness of mind review these sentiments, and honourably recant them.

V.

VOTES OF THE BISHOPS.

No. 1.
29th June, 1868.—Irish Church Suspensory Bill, 2nd reading.

The Bishops' Votes.

			For.	Against.
*		Archbishop of Canterbury (*Longley*)	—	1
*		,, York (*Thomson*)	—	1
*		,, Armagh (*Beresford*)	—	1
		Bishop of Bangor (*Campbell*)	—	1
*	,,	Carlisle (*Waldegrave*)	—	1
	,,	Durham (*Baring*)	—	1
	,,	Ely (*Browne*)	—	1
	,,	Gloucester and Bristol (*Ellicott*)	—	1
*	,,	Killaloe, &c.	—	1
*	,,	Kilmore, &c.	—	1
	,,	Lichfield (*Selwyn*)	—	1
*	,,	Lincoln (*Jackson*)	—	1
	,,	Llandaff (*Ollivant*)	—	1
	,,	London (*Tait*)	—	1
	,,	Manchester (*Lee*)	—	1
*	,,	Meath (*Brabazon*)	—	1
*	,,	Oxford (*Wilberforce*)	—	1
	,,	Ripon (*Bickersteth*)	—	1
	,,	Rochester (*Claughton*)	—	1
*	,,	Salisbury (*Hamilton*)	—	1
	,,	Worcester (*Philpott*)	—	1
			Nil.	21

OBSERVATIONS.

In the House of Commons the 2nd reading was carried 22nd May, 1868, by 312
  Against 258

  Majority for the Bill 54

In the House of Lords the Bill was lost on motion for 2nd reading by—Not Contents 192
  Contents 97

  Majority against 2nd reading............... 95

The majority included 21 Bishops.
No Bishop voted in the minority.

From various causes 10 Bishops who voted against the 2nd reading of the Suspensory Bill did not vote at all on the 2nd reading of the Disestablishment Bill, 18th June, 1869.
An asterisk (*) is affixed to the names of those ten.

No. 2.

18th June 1869.—Irish Church Disestablishment and Disendowment Bill—2nd reading.

The Bishops' Votes.

	For.	Against.
Archbishop of Dublin (*Trench*)	—	1
Bishop of Bangor (*Campbell*)	—	1
,, Derry and Raphoe (*Alexander*)	—	1
,, Durham (*Baring*)	—	1
,, Ely (*Browne*)	—	1
,, Gloucester and Bristol (*Ellicott*)	—	1
,, Hereford (*Atlay*)	—	1
,, Lichfield (*Selwyn*)	—	1
,, Llandaff (*Ollivant*)	—	1
,, London (*Jackson*)	—	1
,, Norwich (*Pelham*)	—	1
,, Peterborough (*Magee*)	—	1
,, Ripon (*Bickersteth*)	—	1
,, Rochester (*Claughton*)	—	1
,, Tuam (*Bernard*)	—	1
,, Worcester (*Philpott*)	—	1
,, St. David's (*Thirlwall*)	1	—
	1	16

For 2nd reading	179
Against do.	146
Majority for 2nd reading	33

OBSERVATIONS.

The Archbishops of Canterbury and York retired behind the Throne, and did not vote.

The votes of each given subsequently were opposed to the Government Bill on every occasion.

The Bishop of Oxford's absence was thus explained by the Bishop of St. David's:—

" My Lords, I cannot refrain from regretting that a most unfor-
" tunate accident deprived me of the company of my Right Reverend
" Brother (the Bishop of Oxford) in the lobby at the late division,
" but I am delighted to hear that he was *present with me in the*
" *spirit, though not in the flesh.*"

No. 3.

29th June, 1869.—In Committee of the House of Lords the Archbishop of Canterbury moved, in Clause 2, Page 1, Line 27, to leave out the word "one," and insert "two," meaning thereby to enlarge the time for disestablishment from 1871 to 1872.

The Bishops' Votes.

	For one.	For two.
Archbishop of Canterbury (*Tait*)	—	1
,, Dublin (*Trench*)	—	1
Bishop of Bangor (*Campbell*)	—	1
,, Derry and Raphoe (*Alexander*)	—	1
,, Durham (*Baring*)	—	1
,, Gloucester and Bristol (*Ellicott*)	—	1
,, Llandaff (*Ollivant*)	—	1
,, London (*Jackson*)	—	1
,, Rochester (*Claughton*)	—	1
,, St. David's (*Thirlwall*)	—	1
,, Tuam, &c. (*Bernard*)	—	1
Bishops for one	—	—
	Nil.	11

For Amendment 130
Against do. 74

Majority against Government 50

OBSERVATIONS.

Eleven Bishops voted against the Government and for the Amendment, and succeeded.

Lord Cairns moved, on the 9th July, to change this amendment, and to alter the time for disestablishing to the 1st of May, 1871, and the House so decided; but the House of Commons disagreed with the Lords, and required the first date to be restored. The Lords did not insist on their amendment, the clause was restored intact, and so passed.

No. 4.

1st July, 1869.—In Committee, the Bishop of Peterborough moved that "the Tax on Clerical Incomes, now payable to the Ecclesiastical Commissioners for Ireland," should not be deducted from the amount of compensation.

The Bishops' Votes.

	For.	Against.
Archbishop of Canterbury (*Tait*)	1	—
,, York (*Thompson*)	1	—
,, Dublin (*Trench*)	1	—
Bishop of Bangor (*Campbell*)	1	—
,, Derry and Raphoe (*Alexander*)	1	—
,, Ely (*Browne*)	1	—
,, Gloucester and Bristol (*Ellicott*)	1	—
,, Lichfield (*Selwyn*)	1	—
,, Llandaff (*Ollivant*)	1	—
,, Peterborough (*Magee*)	1	—
,, Rochester (*Claughton*)	1	—
,, St. David's (*Thirlwall*)	1	—
,, Tuam, &c. (*Bernard*)	1	—
	13	Nil.

For the Motion 94
Against do. 50

Majority against Government 44

OBSERVATION.

The Bishops voted in a body against the Government on this point, and virtually gave it as their opinion that the clergy should be exempted from the payment of taxes.

No. 5.

1st July, 1869.—In Committee, the Earl of Carnarvon moved that glebe lands and houses should be given to the Clergy, free from charge.

The Bishops' Votes.

	Contents.	Not Contents.
Archbishop of Canterbury (*Tait*)	—	1
,, York (*Thompson*)	—	1
,, Dublin (*Trench*)	—	1
Bishop of Bangor (*Campbell*)	—	1
,, Chester (*Jacobson*)	—	1
,, Derry and Raphoe (*Alexander*)	—	1
,, Durham (*Baring*)	—	1
,, Ely (*Browne*)	—	1
,, Gloucester and Bristol (*Ellicott*)	—	1
,, Lichfield (*Selwyn*)	—	1
,, Llandaff (*Ollivant*)	—	1
,, London (*Jackson*)	—	1
,, Oxford (*Wilberforce*)	—	1
,, Peterborough (*Magee*)	—	1
,, Rochester (*Claughton*)	—	1
,, St. David's (*Thirlwall*)	—	1
,, Tuam, &c. (*Bernard*)	—	1
For the Government	Nil.	—
	Nil.	17

On original words being put—Contents... 86
Not Contents 155

Majority against Government............... 69

OBSERVATIONS.

The Bishops were generally unanimous on every motion that sought to distribute the property of the Irish Church among the Clergy. They are evidently of the same mind as Tennyson's "Northern Farmer (New Style)," that the golden bond of union is "*proputty, proputty*." Wonderful talisman! whose powerful touch dissolves, as by enchantment, all differences of sentiment on minor points, and draws together into one lobby High Church, Low Church, Broad Church, to vote together against the spoiler.

No. 6.

2nd July, 1869.—In Committee, clause 27, page 13, line 33, Marquis of Salisbury's Motion on Church Endowment.

Bishops' Votes.

	For.	Against.
For Government...	Nil.	—
NOT CONTENT.		
Archbishop of Canterbury (*Tait*).......................	—	1
,, York (*Thompson*)...........................	—	1
,, Dublin (*Trench*)	—	1
Bishop of Bangor (*Campbell*)	—	1
,, Chester (*Jacobson*)	—	1
,, Durham (*Baring*)	—	1
,, Ely (*Browne*)	—	1
,, Gloucester and Bristol (*Ellicott*)	—	1
,, Lichfield (*Selwyn*)	—	1
,, Llandaff (*Ollivant*)	—	1
,, London (*Jackson*)	—	1
,, Oxford (*Wilberforce*)	—	1
,, Peterborough (*Magee*).......................	—	1
,, Rochester (*Claughton*).......................	—	1
,, St. David's (*Thirlwall*).......................	—	1
,, Tuam, &c. (*Bernard*).........................	—	1
	Nil.	16

Question—original words:—
Contents 69
Not Contents 213

Majority against Government................ 144

OBSERVATION.

Episcopal unanimity was again displayed in favour of increased grants of property to the clergy.

No. 7.

2nd July, 1869.—In Committee, Clause 28, Page 14, Line 31— Duke of Cleveland's Amendment for endowing Catholics and Presbyterians—(Question—*that the original words stand part.*)

Bishops' Votes.

	Contents.	Not Content.
Bishop of Chester (*Jacobson*)	1	—
„ Derry and Raphoe (*Alexander*)	1	—
„ Durham (*Baring*)	1	—
„ Llandaff (*Ollivant*)	1	—
„ Tuam, &c. (*Bernard*)	1	—
Archbishop of Canterbury (*Tait*)	—	1
„ York (*Thomson*)	—	1
Bishop of Ely (*Browne*)	—	1
„ Gloucester and Bristol (*Ellicott*)	—	1
„ Lichfield (*Selwyn*)	—	1
„ Oxford (*Wilberforce*)	—	1
„ Peterborough (*Magee*)	—	1
„ Rochester (*Claughton*)	—	1
„ St. David's (*Thirlwall*)	—	1
	5	9

Contents 146
Not Contents 113

Against Endowment 33

Observations.

Nine Protestant Bishops voted for Catholic and Presbyterian Endowment, and five against.

Eight Catholic Peers voted against the motion, and one only (Lord Orford) voted for it.

The decision was reversed on the 12th July by a majority of seven, which was obtained by the votes of seven Bishops; but the House of Commons disagreed with the Amendment, and the House of Lords not insisting on it, it was withdrawn.

No. 8.

5th July, 1869.—In Committee, Archbishop of Canterbury moved that an increase of Glebe land should be given to the clergy (being the *Ulster Glebes*, granted by James I.), estimated by Lord Dufferin at near £1,000,000, and at any rate exceeding £900,000.

Bishops' Votes.

	For.	Against.
For Government	Nil.	—
Archbishop of Canterbury (*Tait*).........................	—	1
,, Dublin (*Trench*)	—	1
Bishop of Bangor (*Campbell*)	—	1
,, Derry and Raphoe (*Alexander*)	—	1
,, Ely (*Browne*)...	—	1
,, Gloucester and Bristol (*Ellicott*)	—	1
,, Hereford (*Atlay*).................................	—	1
,, Lichfield (*Selwyn*)	—	1
,, London (*Jackson*)	—	1
,, Peterborough (*Magee*).........................	—	1
,, St. David's (*Thirlwall*)	—	1
,, Tuam, &c. (*Bernard*)	—	1
	Nil.	12

Contents 105
Not Contents 55

Against Government 50

The amendment was rejected by 344 to 240 in the House of Commons, and the House of Lords did not insist on it.

No. 9.

5th July, 1869.—In Committee, the Earl of Limerick moved to deduct from the sale of tithe rent-charges for poor rates—(Question—*original words to stand part.*)

Bishops' Votes.

	For.	Against.
CONTENTS.		
Bishop of Derry and Raphoe	1	—
,, Hereford (*Atlay*)	1	—
,, London (*Jackson*)	1	—
,, Tuam, &c. (*Bernard*)	1	—
NOT CONTENT.		
Bishop of Gloucester and Hereford (*Ellicott*)	—	1
	4	1

Original words—
    Contents 91
    Not Contents 64

    Against Amendment 27

This matter concerned the terms granted to the landlords, not the clergy. It was on this occasion that Lord Salisbury so flippantly and unfeelingly said, that he *would rather the Landlords had the money than the Lunatics.*

No. 10.

5th July, 1869.—In Committee, Lord Fitzwalter moved to leave out Page 21, Line 41, relating to the compensation to Maynooth. (Question—*original words to stand part.*)

Bishops' Votes.

	Contents.	Content.	
Archbishop of	Canterbury (*Tait*)	1	—
,,	York (*Thomson*)	1	—
Bishop of	Gloucester and Bristol (*Ellicott*)	1	—
,,	Hereford (*Atlay*)	1	—
,,	Oxford (*Wilberforce*)	1	—
,,	Peterborough (*Magee*)	1	—
,,	St. David's (*Thirlwall*)	1	—
	Not Content.		
Bishop of Tuam, &c. (*Bernard*)		—	1
		7	1

Contents 146
Not Content 22

Against Amendment 124

OBSERVATIONS.

The Bishops did not open their lips on this occasion, and (with one exception) their votes were fairly given. But that receives its explanation when we mark the course they pursued on "Concurrent Endowment." They have nothing to say against giving the money into clerical hands—to any amount; but apply it to the general benefit of the nation—that is *sacrilege!*

No. 11.

6th July, 1869.—In Committee, Lord Cairns moved an Amendment to Clause 68 to reserve Parliamentary power to apply the surplus, without restricting it to secular purposes.

Bishops' Votes.

	Content.	Not Contents.
CONTENT.		
Bishop of Oxford (*Wilberforce*)	1	—
NOT CONTENTS.		
Archbishop of Canterbury (*Tait*)	—	1
,, York (*Thomson*)	—	1
,, Dublin (*Trench*)	—	1
Bishop of Bangor (*Campbell*)	—	1
,, Derry (*Alexander*)	—	1
,, Ely (*Browne*)	—	1
,, Gloucester and Bristol (*Ellicott*)	—	1
,, Hereford (*Atlay*)	—	1
,, Lichfield (*Selwyn*)	—	1
,, London (*Jackson*)	—	1
,, Rochester (*Claughton*)	—	1
,, St. David's (*Thirlwall*)	—	1
,, Tuam, &c. (*Bernard*)	—	1
	1	13

That the original words stand part of the question—

Contents 90
Not Contents 160

Majority against Government.............. 70

OBSERVATIONS.

The House of Commons disagreed to this Amendment.

The House of Lords compromised the difference by removing the words respecting the surplus from the Preamble of the Bill, and transferring them to Section 68th, which fixes the application of the surplus to secular purposes—" *the relief of unavoidable calamity and suffering* "—without strictly defining the form which that relief should take.

Here again the Bishops were all but unanimous in resisting a *really national* use of the surplus funds. The only kind of "calamity and suffering" which seems to move them deeply is *Disendowment.*

No. 12.

9th July, 1869.—On the Report of the Committee, the Marquis of Clanricarde (Lord Somerhill) moved to restore a portion of Clause 28, omitted in Committee, respecting residences of clergy.

Bishops' Votes.

	For.	Against.
For Clause	Nil.	—
NOT CONTENTS.		
Archbishop of Canterbury (*Tait*)	—	1
,, Dublin (*Trench*)	—	1
Bishop of Bangor (*Campbell*)	—	1
,, Derry and Raphoe (*Alexander*)	—	1
,, Lichfield (*Selwyn*)	—	1
,, London (*Jackson*)	—	1
,, Peterborough (*Magee*)	—	1
,, Tuam, &c. (*Bernard*)	—	1
	Nil.	8

Contents 56
Not Contents....................................... 91

Majority against Government 35

OBSERVATIONS.

The object of the motion was to restore the latter part of Clause 28, which required payment of the building charges on Glebe Houses by the new Church.

The Bishops opposed the motion, as usual in such cases.

No. 18.

12th July, 1869.—3rd reading, the Earl of Devon moved to rescind the clause for continuing to the Irish Bishops seats in the House of Lords for their lives.

Bishops' Votes.

	For Motion.	Against.
For Motion	Nil.	—
NOT CONTENTS.		
Archbishop of Canterbury (*Tait*)........................	—	1
Bishop of Ely (*Browne*)	—	1
,, Gloucester and Bristol (*Ellicott*)	—	1
,, Lichfield (*Selwyn*)	—	1
,, Peterborough (*Magee*)........................	—	1
,, Rochester (*Claughton*)	—	1
	Nil.	6

On original words—
    Contents 82
    Not Contents 108

    Majority for Government clause............. 26

OBSERVATIONS.

The absurdity of continuing their seats to the Irish Bishops, after disestablishing the Irish Church, as the House of Lords previously decided, was too manifest, and this motion of a Conservative Peer succeeded. But the Bishops were unanimous in claiming for their brethren this empty and burdensome honour. They feared probably the effect of the precedent to themselves. The vacancy on the Bench, when the Irish Bishops had retired, might be too suggestive.

No. 14.

12th July, 1869.—Third Reading.—Earl Stanhope moved to restore the Endowment of Roman Catholic Clergy and Presbyterian Ministers (rejected on the Duke of Cleveland's motion, 2nd July).

Bishops' Votes.

	Against.	For.
NOT CONTENTS.		
Bishop of Norwich (*Pelham*)	1	—
,, Tuam, &c. (*Alexander*)	1	—
CONTENTS.		
The Archbishop of Canterbury (*Tait*)	—	1
,, York (*Thomson*)	—	1
Bishop of Ely (*Browne*)	—	1
,, Gloucester and Bristol (*Ellicott*)	—	1
,, Lichfield (*Selwyn*)	—	1
,, Peterborough (*Magee*)	—	1
,, Rochester (*Claughton*)	—	1
	2	7

Contents 121
Not Contents 114

Majority for Endowment, and against Government 7

OBSERVATIONS.

Seven Protestant Bishops gave the casting vote in favour of this Endowment of the *Roman Catholic Clergy.*

The Commons rejected the amendment, and the House of Lords did not insist on it.

The Bishop of Oxford and the Bishop of St. David's were absent; the former owing to another "most unfortunate accident."

Thirty-two Peers who voted *against* this endowment on 2nd July were absent from this unexpected division.

No. 15.

20th July 1869.—Consideration of disagreements of the House of Commons to the Amendments in the House of Lords—Earl Granville moved that the House do not insist on Amendment of Preamble.

Bishops' Votes.

	For.	Against.
CONTENT.		
Bishop of Oxford (*Wilberforce*)	1	—
NOT CONTENTS.		
Archbishop of Canterbury (*Tait*)	—	1
,, York (*Thomson*)	—	1
,, Dublin (*Trench*)	—	1
Bishop of Bangor (*Campbell*)	—	1
,, Derry and Raphoe (*Alexander*)	—	1
,, Gloucester and Bristol (*Ellicott*)	—	1
,, Hereford (*Atlay*)	—	1
,, Lichfield (*Selwyn*)	—	1
,, London (*Jackson*)	—	1
,, Peterborough (*Magee*)	—	1
,, Rochester (*Claughton*)	—	1
,, Tuam, &c. (*Bernard*)	—	1
	1	12

Contents	95
Not Contents	173
Majority against Government	78

OBSERVATIONS.

This division brought on a crisis that might have been serious, and even have caused a collision between the two Houses, and *twelve Bishops voted for it.*

Earl Granville, by tact and unfailing temper, had conducted the Bill for the Government, to the admiration of the House and the country.

He had suffered defeat after defeat without complaining, except that he was painfully conscious the Government had not the confidence of the House.

After this division, he stated he could proceed with the Bill no further until he consulted his colleagues, and moved the adjournment for forty-eight hours, viz., from Tuesday to Thursday.

Next day Lord Cairns waited on Earl Granville and proposed terms equivalent to a surrender of all the objectionable amendments, which the House confirmed.

No. 15—*Continued*.

The humiliation was great, but the Bishops were deaf to all warnings, and voted against Government with almost unanimous obstinacy. No thanks to them that the affairs of the country were not plunged into confusion, classes arrayed against each other in bitter strife, and the hopes of the Irish people defeated. And all for what? The mere chance of delaying Disendowment a little longer, or keeping a little more of the beloved *property*.

No. 16.

22nd July, 1869.—Consideration of disagreements of the House of Commons.—Earl Granville moved that the House do not insist on the Amendment to Clause 27 (enactments with respect to Ecclesiastical residences.)—The Archbishop of Dublin said *the sum of money involved was small, but at whatever inconvenience to the House, he must divide upon it.*

Bishops' Votes.

	Content.	Not Contents.
CONTENT.		
Bishop of Chester (*Jacobson*)	1	.
NOT CONTENTS.		
Archbishop of Dublin (*Trench*)	—	1
Bishop of Derry and Raphoe (*Alexander*)	—	1
,, Lichfield (*Selwyn*)	—	1
,, Tuam, &c. (*Bernard*)	—	1
	1	4

Contents 47
Not Contents 17
Majority for Government 30

OBSERVATIONS.

It is satisfactory to recognise the Bishop of Chester (once a Dissenting Minister) favourable to Government on this occasion.

But it is painfully sad to mark the last expiring effort of the Archbishop to snatch one little chestnut out of the fire. *It was but a small sum*, said his Grace. Then why be so obstinately bent on lowering his just dignity for a trifle? When we remember the delightful impressions we have received from the many admirable writings of Richard Chenevix Trench, and the pure and lofty principles advocated in them, and then call up the image of the mournful Prelate stretching out his hand for this " small sum"—*in vain*, we sigh to think how the spirit of a man and a Christian may be extinguished by a Mitre!

Comparison of Nos. 7 and 14.

The Bishops who voted 2nd July, 1869, on the Motion of the Duke of Cleveland to endow Catholics and Presbyterians in Ireland.

Peers.

Against Catholic, &c., endowment.........	146
For ditto......................................	113
Majority against ditto.......................	33

For Catholic Endowment.

The Archbishop of Canterbury	... ...	(*Tait.*)
,, York	... ...	(*Thomson.*)
The Bishop of Ely	... ...	(*Browne.*)
,, Gloucester and Bristol	...	(*Ellicott.*)
,, Lichfield	... ...	(*Selwyn.*)
* ,, Oxford	... ...	(*Wilberforce.*)
,, Peterborough	... ...	(*Magee.*)
,, Rochester	... ...	(*Claughton.*)
* ,, St. David's	... .	(*Thirlwall.*)

—9 Bishops.

Against.

The Bishop of Chester	... ...	(*Jacobson.*)
,, Derry and Raphoe	... ...	(*Alexander.*)
,, Durham	... ...	(*Baring.*)
,, Llandaff	... ...	(*Ollivant.*)
,, Tuam, &c.	... ...	(*Bernard.*)

—5 Bishops.

On the 12th July, 1869, on Earl Stanhope's motion, the Bishop of Norwich (Pelham) voted against, and so did Tuam.

The Bishops whose names have an asterisk (*) affixed did not vote on the Earl of Stanhope's Motion, 12th July. On that occasion the following were

Absent.

The Archbishop of Dublin	... ...	(*Trench.*)
The Bishop of Bangor	... ...	(*Campbell.*)
,, Bath and Wells	... ...	(*Lord Auckland.*)
,, Chichester	... ...	(*Gilbert.*)
,, Exeter	... ...	(*Philpotts.*)
,, Carlisle	... ...	(*Waldegrave.*)
,, Hereford	... ...	(*Atlay.*)
,, Lincoln	... ...	(*Wordsworth.*)
,, London	... ...	(*Jackson.*)
,, Manchester	... ...	(*Lee.*)
,, Ripon	... ...	(*Bickersteth.*)
,, Salisbury	... ...	(*Hamilton.*)
,, St. Asaph	... ...	(*Short.*)
,, Winchester	... ...	(*Sumner.*)
,, Worcester	... ...	(*Philpott.*)

SUMMARY OF BISHOPS' VOTES.

No.		For.	Against.
1	Suspensory Bill, 1868...	—	21
	GOVERNMENT BILL AND CLAUSES, 1869.	For Government.	Against Government.
2	Disestablishment and Disendowment Bill, 2nd reading	1	16
3	Archbishop of Canterbury's Motion (1st Jan., 1872)...	—	16
4	Bishop of Peterboro's Motion (taxes on Clerical Income)	—	13
5	Earl of Carnarvon's Motion (Glebe lands)................	—	17
6	Marquis of Salisbury's Motion (Endowment).............	—	16
7	Duke of Cleveland's Motion (Catholic, &c., Endowment)	5	9
8	Archbishop of Canterbury (Ulster Glebes)................	—	12
9	Earl of Limerick's Motion (Poors' Rates)	1	4
10	Lord Fitzwalter's Motion	1	7
11	Lord Cairns' Motion (on Surplus clause 68).............	1	13
12	Marquis of Clanricarde (to restore part of clause 28)...	—	8
13	The Earl of Devon's Motion (Against Seats for Irish Bishops)	—	6
14	The Earl of Stanhope's Motion (Endowment of Catholics, &c.)..	2	7
15	The Earl of Granville's Motion (Not to insist on Preamble Amendment)	1	12
16	The Archbishop of Dublin's Division against Earl Granville's Motion (Clause 27)............................	1	4
		13	181
			13
			168

The Archbishops of England and Ireland voted uniformly, when present, against Government, and also against the Suspensory Bill.

Both English Archbishops voted for Endowment of Catholics and Presbyterians in the two divisions. The Archbishop of Dublin was absent.

Six Bishops voted against Catholic Endowment, and *nine* (including the English Archbishops) in favour of it.

The Bishops of Oxford and St. David's voted for the Duke of Cleveland's motion, but were absent from the division on Earl Stanhope's, for Catholic Endowment.

VI.

VOTES OF CATHOLIC PEERS

On the Second Reading of the Irish Church Bill.

Peers.	
Duke of Norfolk	For
Earl Denbigh	,,
,, Fingall	,,
,, Granard	,,
,, Orford	,,
,, Gainsborough	,,
,, Dunraven	Absent
Marquis Bute	,,
Lord Camoys	For
,, Stourton	,,
,, Vaux	,,
,, Petre	,,
,, Arundel	,,
,, Stafford	,,
,, Clifford	,,
,, Lovat	,,
,, Dormer	Absent
,, Beaumont	,,
Viscount Gormanston	,,
Earl of Kenmore	,,

14 For, 6 Absent; None Against.

VOTES OF CATHOLIC PEERS

On Concurrent Endowment. Session 1869.

Peers.	Duke of Cleveland's Amendment.	Earl Stanhope's Amendment.
Duke of Norfolk	Against	Absent
Earl Denbigh	,,	For
,, Fingall	,,	Against
,, Granard	,,	,,
,, Orford	For	Absent
,, Gainsborough	Absent	,,
,, Dunraven	,,	,,
Marquis of Bute	,,	,,
Lord Camoys	Against	Against
,, Stourton	Absent	Absent
,, Vaux	,,	,,
,, Petre	,,	Against
,, Arundell	,,	For
,, Stafford	Against	Absent
,, Clifford	,,	,,
,, Lovat	Absent	,,
,, Dormer	,,	,,
,, Beaumont	,,	,,
Viscount Gormanston	,,	,,
Earl of Kenmore	,,	,,
	7 Against	4 Against
	1 For	2 For
	12 Absent	14 Absent

Concurrent Endowment in the Commons.

The only occasion upon which Concurrent Endowment was formally under discussion in the Commons was on May 7th, upon Mr. Pim's motion that the surplus of Irish Church property should be devoted to the building of Glebe houses, first for Episcopalian Clergy, next for Roman Catholic Priests, and lastly for the Presbyterian Ministers. After a long debate Mr. Pim ultimately withdrew his motion.

Mr. Pim is reputed to be a Quaker.

Mr. Disraeli gave notice of an Amendment, involving the principle of Concurrent Endowment, but it was not moved.

VII.

QUOTATIONS OF CHURCHMEN'S OPINIONS.

It may be well to give a few quotations in support of the assertions made in the Introductory Review regarding the strong dissatisfaction felt by members of the Church of England with the conduct of the Bishops in advocating " Concurrent Endowment," as well as to show the growth of opinion in the same quarter in favour of their retirement from the House of Lords. These will also serve to make it clear that the proposal to relieve them from their Parliamentary duties is not the offspring of sectarian jealousy, but springs from an enlightened zeal for the true interests both of the Church and of the nation.

1. From a pamphlet on *"Concurrent Endowment, and its Episcopal Patrons, by a Clergyman of the Church of England:"—*

" Who that remembers the speeches at St. James's Hall, in the spring of 1868—whose mind does not bound on to the reflection, when dwelling on the speeches delivered in the House of Peers, in the summer of 1869,

'Oh! what a falling off was there, my countrymen!'

Some mystery may even underlie the strange phenomenon that highly-placed and well-educated men should so deliberately go out of their way to be wicked; while those who represent the Roman Catholic Hierarchy seem—so far as man can judge—honourably, honestly, and faithfully flinging back the proffered gift of palatial residences and parsonages, with scorn and contempt, into the faces of those who would build such castles in the air." (P. 5.)

The writer closes by saying :—

"We venture to predict that not many years will pass before the Archbishops and Bishops are cast down from their present high estate, and that they will fall unpitied, unforgiven; outcast of England, though not, we trust, of Heaven. For, although the people of England may forgive them when they have fallen, on account of their first vote in the House of Lords on this Endowment question, they can never forget or excuse the repetition of that offence, when they might have rectified the blunder they had made in voting for the Duke of Cleveland's motion, which vote had been condemned, by both friends and foes alike, almost throughout the whole length and breadth of the United Kingdom." (P. 30.)

2. From an admirable pamphlet that came out last year, entitled, "*Church Reform.* NO MORE LORD BISHOPS. *By Lay Church.*" we take the following extract:—

"I verily believe, that from peer to peasant the opinion is forming, and rapidly spreading, and ere long will be uttered in loud and decided tones by the nation, that the time has arrived when Bishops of the Established Church in England should cease wielding a special political power, and should no longer have seats in the House of Lords.

"As a member of the Church of England of upwards of fifty years standing, and belonging to a family which has been Church of England for five generations, I will assert what I know to be the deliberate opinion of many Churchmen, viz,, that the master grievance and heavy burden of that Church, the evil which is the fruitful parent of many other evils, the cause which to a certain extent paralyses religious activity, and obstructs wise and necessary progress, the mainspring of personal pride, and the prime temptation to political intrigue,—that all these centre in, and spring from, that unchristian custom, the hybrid offspring of Papal and feudal times, under which the Bishops of the English Church sit as "LORDS" in the Upper House of Parliament. We declaim against the temporal power of the Pope; but here, in our midst, have we the temporal power of the Heads of our own Church; a power held as tenaciously, and producing results almost as evil and fatal, as that held by the old man at the Vatican."

The pamphlet thus concludes:—

"I believe that the retirement of the Bishops from the House of Lords would be followed by the happiest results; by the sweeping away of various abuses which at present limit the Church's usefulness, and impede its progress in the nation; by an increased activity, and a greater purity in religious matters, and a firmer and deeper hold by the Church on the affections of the people. And I also believe that the Bishops themselves would be among the first to benefit by the change.

"And, therefore, I recommend the subject to the consideration of all thoughtful and independent members of the Church of England, and exclaim from my heart, "Success to Church Reform," and "*No more* LORD *Bishops.*" (P. 34.)

3. In a leading article in the *Church Review*, August 7, 1869, among other very severe and caustic remarks on the character and procedure of those who are now exalted to the Episcopal office, occur the following:—

"Such men are the necessary results of a system created by political exigencies. When a Statesman selects a Bishop, he does it either with a view to gratify his party, or to strengthen it by making a popular appointment, having an eye to safety and sobriety at the same time. * * * Our great grievance is the way in which our Episcopal appointments are made; and it seems likely enough, as far as that point is concerned, that *the first step to a better state of things will be taken when Bishops no longer have a seat in the House of Lords.*"

4. "But the whole discipline of the Church is out of order. *The Bishops are so secularised by their seats in Parliament,* they are such mere servants of the State, nothing can be hoped for from them. The supine suicidal course at present taken by our Bishops will speedily lead to a universal cry for disestablishment, if they do not soon awake to their responsibilities as chief pastors of Christ's Church, rather than merely Church and State overseers."—*A Member of the English Church Union,* in *Church Review,* September 11, 1869.

5. The two preceding quotations express the views of those who may be regarded as High Church and Ritualistic. The earnest desire, however, which they breathe for some decided improvement in the way of greater liberty and activity in the Church, is undeniable. But in the Evangelical section there are many whose aspirations in the same direction, on different principles, are quite as strong, if not stronger. Witness the letters recently addressed to *The Record* on Church Reform, by that eminent and warm-hearted

minister of Christ, the Rev. J. C. Ryle, whose various publications have been read with delight and profit by multitudes outside the pale of the Church Establishment. We quote from a review of these letters that appeared in the January number of the *Liberator* of this year :—

"So far as a reform of the Establishment is concerned, Mr. Ryle may be described as a root-and-branch man. His denunciations are unsparing, his boldness almost audacious, and his remedies, within narrow limits, absolutely heroic. Practically, he would reconstruct the Church of England from top to bottom. Beginning with the Episcopate, he would not only create more bishoprics, but have Bishops of a less autocratic type, would pay them but £2000 a year, would not have them appointed absolutely by the Crown, and would *deprive them of their seats in the House of Lords.*

6. It is probably well known that Archdeacon Denison has declared his willingness to "join with Mr. Hadfield" to obtain the removal of the Bishops from the House of Lords, not because he disapproves of their recent conduct, but "because," he says, "Establishment having been cut away from under our feet, I wish to see all things done which may help towards some realising of the position, and some preparing for the time when the Church of England shall be disestablished."

The late Lord Henley, (brother-in-law of Sir Robert Peel,) in a pamphlet on Church Reform, published many years ago, gave it as his opinion that the retirement of the Bishops from the House of Lords would be the most important and effective step towards the removal of abuses in the Church that had been made since the Reformation.

(For additional opinions of the same kind, see the speech of Mr. C. Lushington, in the Debate of 1837, referred to in page 74.)

CONCLUSION.

Manifestly, then, the minds of men within the Church are ripening for the change. The movement hastens on apace. In the ensuing Session of Parliament Mr. Somerset Beaumont, according to notice, will ask leave to introduce a Bill to relieve the Bishops from attendance in Parliament. Mr. Beaumont is himself an attached member of the Church of England. He is following worthily in the steps of Mr. C. Lushington and others, who, in 1837, brought up the same question and secured a good discussion of it in the House of Commons.* Let all sound Liberals rally round Mr. Beaumont, and support his motion heartily when it is brought forward. Let none flinch or waver from a feeling that present success is out of the question, and that our policy must be one of delay. Constant and fearless attacks on abuses are sure to overcome them at the last. Church rates were not abolished till after many an assault and many a withering exposure. So with the monster iniquity of the Irish Church. Now, these are things of the past. But the lessons taught by these contests and the courage inspired by our success should animate and strengthen us in what we have yet to do. Especially should we be hopeful and courageous when we remember that this is no party conflict;—we seek no triumph for ourselves, no humiliation of others; we strive to win for the whole nation freedom, light and unity. Never can a

* See the Debate on Church Reform and the Bishops' Seats in Parliament, Feb. 16th, 1837, republished by Mr. Hadfield, with an Introduction, discussing the general bearings of the question: Stanford, London, 1867.

nation be truly free while so many of its members are fettered (though by their own fault) in their ecclesiastical relations. True enlightenment is hindered by the lingering shadows of mediæval assumptions. Unity is impossible, so long as unjust privileges are defended. Those who enjoy these privileges are in fact most injured by them. All classes are annoyed by the spectacle of the Bishops in Parliament, and by their obstructive efforts; but it is the Bishops themselves who are seriously damaged. They are the victims of a false position. Surely in some Episcopal minds — now that the turmoil is over—there must be longings for a purer and calmer air, and the joys of a nobler service. Surely they would be glad to leave behind them the strife, the dust, and the shouts of the Parliamentary arena. What might not the eloquence of *Peterborough* do, were it consecrated to the true objects of the Christian ministry, instead of being wasted in futile and inglorious debates? Let his Lordship seek his true renown and his enduring reward in the labours of his diocese, rousing the masses from their irreligious apathy, and kindling the zeal of his brethren:—let him soar like the eagle to the azure fields of heaven, and leave meaner natures, in quarrels over the spoil, to sting like the wasp, or to ravin like the vulture.

It will be a happy day for England when her Bishops shall be—what many desire to see them—*Spiritual Overseers, and nothing else;* defending the faith by their learning, diffusing it by their eloquence, and commending it by their lives—" *giving no offence in anything, that the ministry be not blamed.*" May God speed the coming of that day! Already do we see streaks of its dawn reddening the horizon. Ere long its light will fill the sky.

END.

www.ingramcontent.com/pod-product-compliance
Lightning Source LLC
Chambersburg PA
CBHW020237090426
42735CB00010B/1733